Waterwise Gardening

WATERWISE
Gardening

WATER, PLANTS AND CLIMATE
A PRACTICAL GUIDE

IAN COOKE

NEW HOLLAND

First published in 2008 by
New Holland Publishers (UK) Ltd
London · Cape Town · Sydney · Auckland
Garfield House, 86–88 Edgware Road
London W2 2EA, United Kingdom
www.newhollandpublishers.com

80 McKenzie Street, Cape Town 8001
South Africa

Unit 1, 66 Gibbes Street, Chatswood,
NSW 2067 Australia

218 Lake Road, Northcote, Auckland
New Zealand

ISBN 978 1 84537 985 8

COMMISSIONING EDITOR Clare Sayer
SENIOR EDITOR Emma Pattison
DESIGNER Andrew Barron, Thextension
ILLUSTRATIONS Stephen Dew
PRODUCTION Laurence Poos
EDITORIAL DIRECTION Rosemary Wilkinson

See page 192 for picture credits

10 9 8 7 6 5 4 3 2 1

Printed and bound in Singapore by Tien Wah Press (Pte) Ltd
Reproduction by Pica Digital Pte Ltd, Singapore

Contents

Introduction

The weather is of great importance to gardeners and many seem to be obsessed with it. We are always moaning – it's either too hot, too cold, too wet or too dry, and it is this last situation that forms the basis for this book. Until relatively recently those of us who garden in traditionally cooler and wetter climates did not need to concern ourselves with a lack of water, but weather conditions are changing and in order to be successful gardeners we must learn to become waterwise.

Memories of extreme weather conditions remain firmly lodged in a gardener's mind. Personally, I remember the UK's Great Storms of the 1980s, when many thousands of trees were lost overnight. I recall the shock and horror on the estate where I then worked as I catalogued over 50 mature trees uprooted or wrecked beyond salvage, not to mention numerous wounded trees.

As I complete this book in June 2007, parts of Europe are experiencing severe wet weather and there are many seriously flooded areas with immense property damage and lost lives. This is midsummer and the subject of this book seems like a bad joke. However, just a few weeks ago the same areas passed through the warmest spring on record with virtually no rain. Soils were bone dry and new plantings were being irrigated. Last year seems almost forgotten but in some parts of Europe, 2006 was one of the hottest summers on record with water shortages, hosepipe bans and drought orders imposed in many areas. I recall driving through one city centre in midsummer and observing the planting on the central reservation. It was brown and withered, almost as if blasted by fire, but it was merely responding to the excessive lack of water the area was experiencing.

Looking back over my gardening life the summer of 1975 also springs to mind when there was no mentionable rain in my native UK between March and October. Lawns burnt out rapidly, plants scorched in the heat and eventually mature trees went into early leaf fall. Two years earlier the nation's gardeners had bravely embraced a new initiative with 'Plant a Tree 73', followed by 'Plant Some More 74'. As the summer of 75 started to bake, the phrase 'Keep 'em Alive 75' was coined, followed cynically by 'Bundle of Sticks 76' as we cleared away the dead remnants of our earlier optimistic plantings. All scorched up through heat and a lack of moisture.

Whether or not we accept the predictions of global warming, it does seem crystal clear that gardeners will need to learn how to garden with extreme weather conditions. One of the most challenging of these is limited water.

RIGHT A wealth of colour including Californian poppies in the desert garden at the Old Vicarage, East Ruston, UK.

SECTION ONE
Waterwise fundamentals

What's changing

Gardens and the act of gardening give great pleasure to millions of people all over the world, whether as a weekend pastime, a serious hobby or a chosen career path. So when weather and climate change starts to affect our activities, it affects many people. Many gardeners are experiencing the effects of global warming as extremes of weather conditions, and are finding that traditional plants and planting schemes are no longer suitable for today's climate.

Learning from others

As we start to consider gardening with minimum water, whether it be from rain or from stored sources, gardeners are embarking on a relatively new set of conditions in which to garden. Many of the plants we grow come from climates where water is not in short supply and so have in the past adapted well to our climate. Now with drier summers and water shortages, they rapidly show stress.

Many countries have long addressed these issues. I travel regularly to California where rainfall is low and summer temperatures soar above the 100's. Most of the plantings are either irrigated or are planned as desert-style landscapes. They are all designed for heat and drought. Many gardens, public landscapes and even grass verges have an automatic irrigation system. In walking the footpaths in a public area, you can sometimes be startled as the irrigation cuts in to keep public grass areas green and lush. Irrigation is as much a basic specification as frost protection is in cooler climates. This is of course dependant on abundant supplies of water for such irrigation.

Xeriscaping

The alternative to intensive irrigation is to base our gardening culture on a minimum use of water, and many areas of the world have chosen to take this direction. In the USA, the term xeriscape is sometimes used. It quite simply means landscaping in ways and with plants that do not require additional water. The idea was developed in Denver as long ago as 1981 and the term is trade-marked with its own logo. Adopting xeriscaping essentially means using plants that have minimal water requirements and adapting traditonal gardening techniques to conserve water.

Xeriscaping has many advantages, not the least of which is that it is environmentally responsible. More water is available for other essential uses and, where water is charge-able, costs are lower. Xeriscape gardening is usually low maintenance, leaving the gardener time to relax and be lazy during hot weather. Carefully chosen xeriscape plants remain healthy and colourful during times of water stress, meaning gardens do not fade in hot weather. Many of these plants will also attract bees, butterflies and other wildlife.

No system is without disadvantages and xeriscaping has a few, too. Initially it needs a thoroughly new mind-set to embrace new ideas, changed techniques and different plants. Traditional gardeners may find this difficult. Some well loved features such as emerald green lawns may not be achievable in quite the same way and it may no longer be possible to grow favourite plants. Initial preparation for new plantings must be thorough and extensive. If gardeners opt to use some water, an efficient irrigation system must be used that will not waste valuable water. This may be expensive and time consuming to install.

Weather patterns

The summer of 2006 was hot and dry. In many areas the average temperatures for 2006 were higher than at any time since records began in 1659. Globally, it looks set to be the sixth hottest year on record. Several recent winters have been dry and rainfall levels have been at their lowest since 1933.

BELOW Extremes of weather can have devasting effects, such as the aftermath of the Great Storms in the UK during the 1980s.

However, by the end of January 2007 the UK had experienced twice the average rainfall and the second mildest January since 1914, and much of Northern Europe was experiencing similar conditions. The reservoirs and underground aquifers were fortunately filling but the ground was too saturated to do any cultivations. These areas also experienced a number of extremely stormy days with wind speeds up to 80 mph. If that wasn't enough, the wet late winter turned rapidly into an early summer with a hot dry spring where temperatures again exceeding all records for similar times of the year. Then the summer bought floods...

DEFINITION OF DROUGHT

So what is drought? Drought is defined as a period of time when there is not enough water to support farming, urban, human, and environmental water needs. A drought usually refers to an extended period of below-normal rainfall, but can also be caused by drying-up of water storage areas such as reservoirs, boreholes or lakes. What may be considered as normal rainfall will vary from one area of the world to another. Drought may be a feature of nearly all the world's climatic regions. The effects of drought vary greatly, depending on the area's water needs.

Drought will first be determined as a meteorological phenomenon when rainfall drops below averages for an extended period of time. It becomes an agricultural drought when there is insufficient water to raise crops usually grown in the area. It then becomes a hydrological drought when there is insufficient water in reservoirs for normal urban usage. On a large scale drought may lead to famine, fire, disease and considerable widespread hardship.

Even though scientists may argue about what is happening, it seems clear that in the latter half of the 20th century we have seen distinct climate changes across many parts of the world. The winter of 1962/63 was notable for its severity, killing many plants that we thought were hardy. The drought of 1976 made us aware of the problems of acute water shortage. In 1987 and 1990 hurricanes caused devastation across southern parts of the UK with the loss of many trees and in 2001 many areas of the country were subject to flooding.

Climate change

Scientists have made numerous predictions as to what our climate will be like in twenty, fifty and a hundred years, but what is more immediate is the observation that climate changes have increased the growing season we now experience. Milder and shorter winters mean that plants come into growth and flower earlier in the spring and continue to grow further into the winter. Almost any gardener will have observed that it is no longer possible to put the lawn-mower away in the autumn and start raking leaves. Grass continues to grow (albeit more slowly) right through our milder winters and leaves do not drop until we get a frost in the coldest parts of winter. Those of us who have been gardening for a lifetime are having to rethink the way we do a number of traditional tasks and the seasons when we do them.

Climate change poses a number of major problems for gardeners. In particular coping with the extremes of winter waterlogging at one end and summer drought at the other.

RIGHT Plants in deserts have adapted to allow them to store water during shortages and yet still present an amazingly lush appearance.

Careful culture can help overcome many of these challenges. Alongside the problems, global warming does offer the gardener the opportunity to garden in an extended growing season and to experiment with a whole host of new and exciting plants.

The World's dry climates

Many parts of the world experience dry climates. These occur in every continent including parts of Europe. Natural dry environments come in many forms: deserts, grass prairies, shrublands, open woodlands and savannas. Although these differ in topography, climate, vegetation and wildlife, they have many common factors. They generally have more sunny days than cloudy ones and are likely to receive less than 51 cm (20 in) rainfall a year. They will be likely to lose their moisture quickly to evaporation and experience high temperatures and low humidity.

Deserts

Deserts occur in a number of parts of the world and probably cover as much as 20 per cent of its surface. Those that we are interested in here have characteristically bright sunshine, high temperatures and a lack of water, be it rain, snow, dew or fog. Such areas may be a long way from the coast, in the rain shadow of a mountain range or where the soil is unfavourable or unstable.

Most deserts will have high daytime temperatures, but because there is no cloud cover the night time temperatures may plummet. Frost may occur on occasions and some of the annual precipitation may be through snow. This means that many desert plants will be frost hardy. The key characteristic that is of interest to us here is the lack of moisture that causes these areas to be arid landscapes.

Not all of the world's deserts are hot. Some desert areas are known as cold deserts, for example the Antarctic. They tend to have long cold winters and short summers, and plant life is limited or non-existent. Due to the lack of plants cold deserts are of less interest than hot deserts to us here.

Grasslands

Grasslands vary greatly although the predominant vegetation is grass. Trees are generally absent or only present alongside waterways or on hillsides. Grasslands are also often called prairies and have given rise to a particular style of mixed garden planting that features a high proportion of grasses. Grasslands are naturally classified as short, mixed or tall, according to the amount of rain they receive. As well as grasses many other wildflowers grow in these areas, such as asters, golden rod, penstemons and globeflowers.

Shrublands

Shrublands are not really plant communities on their own but are often adjacent to either deserts or grasslands where conditions are slightly different, with either shelter or a little additional water. For example a river running through a grassland will have a shrubland environment alongside its banks. These are given different names in varying parts of the world. You may hear of the Chaparral, which is a shrubland plant community found primarily in California, USA, and in the Cape region of South African these areas are known as fynbos.

Open woodlands, savannah and parklands

These are all communities of trees but not true forests as such. Open woodlands will consist of small trees, usually separately spaced, with species such as pine, cypress and yucca. These areas are often the transition phase between desert shrublands and mountainous forests. Savanna and parkland are similar but with the trees widely spaced and large tracts of grasses and wildflowers between. Trees will include oaks, pines and juniper.

Mediterranean regions

The region around the Mediterranean Sea has a climate of mild, rainy winters and hot, dry summers. This distinctive climate pattern is also found in four other widely separated parts of the world, namely California, Chile, South Africa and Australia. Even in countries never in the past been seen as having a Mediterranean climate the prevailing weather patterns in the last few years has become a lot closer, meaning that gardeners in these regions need to think more along the lines of the Mediterranean garden. Whilst we may look to hot climates and even desert landscape for inspiration, climates with warm, wet autumns bringing relief to parched gardens are more akin to the Mediterranean than the Californian desert.

BELOW A typical prairie landscape with a profusion of grasses and other native flowers which give a verdant appearance but grow with minimal rainfall.

Water issues

All gardeners will undoubtedly realize the importance of water for plants and the close link with water in the soil. However until water is in short supply we are often not aware of quite how critical it is for the success of our gardens. In order to approach a responsible use of water, it is helpful to look in detail at what happens to water in soil and in plants and how it gets from one to the other.

Water in plants

Water is essential to life on earth and this of course includes plants. Many plants or parts of plants contain up to 90 per cent water so you will see how vital this is to their survival and growth. Water is essential for a number of key functions in a plant. The most basic of these is turgidity – the process which enables the plant to stay upright and display its leaves and flowers at the correct angle to the light. When a plant is short of water it wilts because there is insufficient water to maintain turgidity. We have all seen blow-up Christmas decorations which lose their air, deflate and collapse in a heap on the ground – without water, a plant is similar and loses it correct shape and form. It is not quite so dramatic with a plant, as many plants have woody cells which enable them to retain most of their shape and stature, but the soft green, water filled parts, like leaves and shoot tips, collapse.

Water is also a key component in the essential process of photosynthesis, which is the means by which plants grow. Plants have the unique ability to use water, sunlight and carbon dioxide from the air to make sugars, which are the basic building blocks for new growth. Therefore when plants are short of water, photosynthesis slows or stops and the growth processes are reduced. Commercial growers, who need to produce the maximum yields from crops of fruit and vegetables, will endeavour to supply the critical amounts of water at key times in a crop's lifecycle to maximize the yield and the resulting profit.

Plants also use water for the transport of food materials throughout the plant. Any nutrients that the plant takes from the soil are absorbed as a solution dissolved in water. This solution of nutrients within water is passed throughout the plant by various processes such as osmosis. This is simply the way in which nutrients pass from cell to cell through the plant in an organized way, enabling the plant to transfer what it needs to the areas where new growth is taking

RIGHT The Abbey Gardens on Tresco, with their many exotic plants, are the nearest to a Mediterranean garden that will be found in the UK.

place. These will be the growing points at the top of the stems, new roots and structures such as flowers and fruits. So again, restricted water will reduce the growth of the plant.

This is also closely linked with the transpiration stream, which is the means by which a plant loses water primarily from its leaves but also from its other green parts. It is a complex process during which the leaves open pores, called stomata, in order to let in carbon dioxide, which we have already learnt is essential. At the same time water vapour is released from the plant. As the water is lost more is pulled up through the plant from the roots and as it does, it not only transports the nutrients around the plant but acts as a cooling system, keeping the plant at an even temperature on warm days.

The rate of transpiration is linked to temperature, light and wind. So in high temperatures or windy conditions the transpiration stream will slow to protect the plant. Although very efficient and adaptable, plants cannot cope with extreme conditions such as heatwave weather. If water is in short supply, the plant will lose more water than it can absorb and wilting takes place. When this happens, other processes such as photosynthesis start to shut down and growth slows or stops.

All plants have preferences for the amount of water they require, from aquatic plants at one extreme through to desert plants at the opposite end of the water spectrum. Every plant will have ideal conditions for growth, neither too wet, nor too dry. Many of the ordinary plants that we traditionally grow in our gardens come from areas where there is no real shortage of water. In the past with regular summer rainfall we have been able to grow a very wide range of plants successfully. However when we experience an unexpected drought and the supply of mains water is restricted, we then see how critical it is for plants to have the correct amounts of water.

At the very least, water-stressed plants will slow in their growth and the full stature of plants and potential leaf size will not be achieved. Flowering or cropping will often be

ROOTS AND MYCORRHIZA
The majority of water that plants absorb is taken up by the root system from the soil. The all important roots are the very fine ones with their extensions called root hairs. These are very delicate and easily damaged, which is why gardeners often emphasize the importance of handling plants gently when transplanting. Developing a good root system is essential for all healthy plants but particularly so when we are looking critically at water uptake.

As well as roots, some plants live in association with beneficial fungi called mycorrhiza. These are composed of numerous very fine thread-like structures which are attached to roots and also able to function like roots absorbing water. Mycorrhiza are therefore able to aid their host plants in the absorption of the water from the soil. Some trees and specialist plants such as orchids naturally have mycorrhiza but experimental work is suggesting that a more widespread use of the fungi may help plants living in water-stressed soils. Products are now available for the home gardener containing mycorrhizal fungi and anyone embarking on a planting project in hostile conditions might consider this as one way of enhancing establishment.

delayed or can occur prematurely with a reduced yield. In the short term leaves will wilt, although they may return to their normal state overnight. Some plants, such as the tall Lobelias, will wilt but when they recover have a permanent and unsightly kink in their stems.

When water stress is coupled with the high temperatures we experience in a heatwave, the effect on the plant can be more drastic. Leaves will scorch and turn brown, growth will die back. Plants may also divert more energies to root production in an effort to utilise what water is available so growth will seem even less. Under such circumstances it is likely that the plants will be susceptible to various pests and diseases, which will take advantage of their weakened state.

Prolonged drought and high temperatures may result in the death of some plants. Woody plants are less likely to be so affected because they can drop all of their leaves prematurely and go into an early dormancy, much to their advantage. The woody structure of a mature tree or shrub will usually have enough resources within its tissues to remain alive until conditions once again become favourable to their survival. Small annuals, herbaceous plants or vegetables have no such long-term resources and will rapidly

decline and die. Annuals in particular are likely to complete their flowering rapidly and go into seed production in an effort to perpetuate themselves. It is in this context that we speak of vegetables 'bolting' and running rapidly to seed, usually making them unusable as a crop and therefore unsuitable for sale or consumption.

BELOW Water is essential for many functions throughout the plant and without it a green plant will very rapidly start to fail.

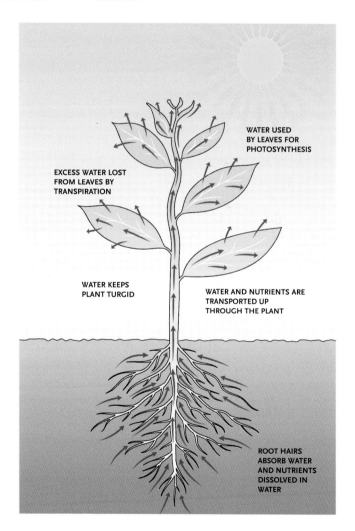

WATER USED BY LEAVES FOR PHOTOSYNTHESIS

EXCESS WATER LOST FROM LEAVES BY TRANSPIRATION

WATER KEEPS PLANT TURGID

WATER AND NUTRIENTS ARE TRANSPORTED UP THROUGH THE PLANT

ROOT HAIRS ABSORB WATER AND NUTRIENTS DISSOLVED IN WATER

THE SPONGE ANALOGY

Understanding the water in a soil can be helped by considering a simple bath sponge. When dropped in a bucket of water the sponge becomes saturated just like soil in a rain storm. When we pick the sponge out of the water and hold it loosely in the air, the excess water will drain out until it stops dripping. This is just like a soil when it drains after raining but is still fully charged with water available to plants. Now if we squeeze that sponge, lots more water will come out and this simulates the removal of water by plants. The harder we squeeze the more difficult it becomes to remove more water and this is again similar to what plants experience as a soil dries. Finally you will be unable to squeeze any more drops out but if you touch the sponge to your face, it will feel damp – there is still some water there but it is held too strongly for removal. This is just like a soil that has dried and at that stage plants will wilt.

Water in the soil

Although plants can absorb small quantities of water through their leaves, the majority of a plant's water supply comes from the soil. For this reason it is important to consider how the soil holds, stores and releases water. Different types of soil hold differing amounts of water and the way they are cultivated and treated will also affect water retention. It is all dependant on the pore space – the gaps between the crumbs of soil. These gaps are critical as they provide room for both air and water in the soil, both of which are vital for healthy plant growth.

Soils are made up of a mix of sand silt and clay in varying proportions, and a good mixed soil with a balance of all of these will be called a loam. Sandy soils have the largest individual spaces between them but, strangely, do not hold the greatest amount of water. It's is the clay proportion of the soil with the smallest pores that is able to hold the most water.

The amount of moisture that a soil can hold is also determined by its structure. This is a tricky concept to grasp but is all to do with the way the soil has been treated by cultivation or other means. A properly cultivated soil that has been handled carefully at the right seasons will appear crumbly, be easy to work and will hold large quantities of water in its pore spaces. A badly treated soil that has been cultivated when wet, perhaps, or compacted with heavy machinery will have had all the pore spaces squashed out of it, and although it may appear to be wet will actually have a poor water holding capacity. This would be said to have poor structure.

When it rains or we irrigate the soil all the pores, large and small, initially become filled with water and the soil becomes saturated. When the rain or irrigation stops, the excess water runs away, leaving the soil fully charged with as much water as it can hold in its smaller pores. The water runs away from the larger pores leaving air spaces, which are also essential. This stage, when there is both a generous amount of water and air within the soil, is the ideal for maximum plant growth. Farmers and commercial growers will try to keep the soil at this stage for the greatest amount of time to maximize growth and yield. It is technically known as field capacity.

As plants grow they remove water from the soil until a stage is reached when they cannot remove any more and the plant will become stressed and wilt. During this process the water is held by the soil and it becomes increasingly difficult for the plant's roots to remove it as it is held firmly by electrical charges on the clay particles. This ability to attract water by electrical charges is another reason why clay soils hold more water.

Soils will also lose water from their surface simply through evaporation into the air. This water is of course lost and can no longer be available to plants. High summer temperatures and also windy weather will encourage such water loss. This can be reduced by covering the soil with some material that stops the water evaporating. We call this process mulching and it is an important technique in water conservation that we will discuss in Section Two (see pages 33–41).

If excess water cannot drain away after rain or irrigation, the soil is said to be waterlogged. This may be because the soil is compacted or damaged in some way or because the water table is to high. The water table is the natural level of water within all soils. In many situations this will be way below the surface of the soil but in some locations this may be near enough to the surface to become apparent. Moisture is capable of rising within a soil from the water table by means of

capillary action – this is like the effect of a wick or a piece of fabric dropped in a puddle that soaks up the water. Some soils with a high clay content may be able to suck up water from the water table up to 2 m (2 yd) below the surface of the soil, so you will see the importance of clay in a soil to help retain moisture.

BELOW Soils with a high clay content hold far more water than sandy soils and so will help plants to thrive in dry spells.

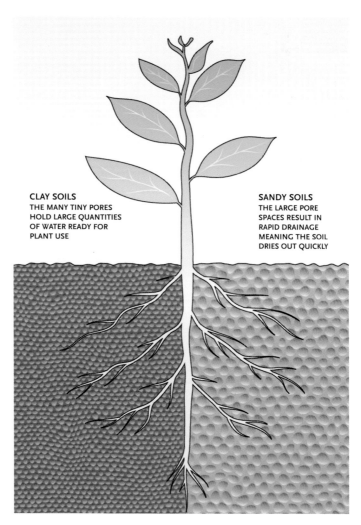

CLAY SOILS
THE MANY TINY PORES
HOLD LARGE QUANTITIES
OF WATER READY FOR
PLANT USE

SANDY SOILS
THE LARGE PORE
SPACES RESULT IN
RAPID DRAINAGE
MEANING THE SOIL
DRIES OUT QUICKLY

Water sources

The main basic source of water is, of course, precipitation; rain, snow, hail and sleet. When water reaches the ground some will run off into drains, streams and rivers but much will be absorbed into the soil. This filters down and eventually reaches underlying rocks where it collects in the pore spaces. This natural reservoir is known as an aquifer and its level is the water table. The water we use is sourced in a number of ways but the main supplies come from these natural aquifers deep in the soil. Some also comes from man-made reservoirs and to a certain extent from rivers.

The legislation and governance of water supplies throughout the world is complex and in some outdated as far as gardens are concerned. There are three agencies involved in the governance of water in the UK.

Defra (The Department for Environment, Food and Rural Affairs) has a duty to ensure that the public water supply is maintained and that the environment isn't damaged. The Department's formal role when water is under stress is to deal with drought order applica-

tions made to the Secretary of State. Defra has policy responsibility for the legislation that governs water resources and which includes the law relating to hosepipe bans, drought permits and drought orders.

Secondly there is *The Environment Agency*, which is the statutory body that has a duty to manage water resources in England and Wales. Its aim is to ensure that the management and future development of our water resources is carried out in a sustainable manner. Drought Permits are granted by the Environment Agency.

Finally the regional *Water Companies* are the commercial organizations that actually provide the water. They have the power to impose temporary sprinkler and hosepipe bans that prohibit or restrict the use of water for private gardens. Hosepipe bans do not require the approval of the Government or the Environment Agency.

In most areas of the UK, water is charged as a standard fee based on the rateable value of the property. Under normal seasonal conditions, garden watering is included, although some of the water companies levy an additional fee for the use of hosepipe and sprinkler. A hosepipe license does not give you an exemption when there is a hosepipe ban or drought order in place, although you may get a refund. All new properties since 1989 have been fitted with water meters when built. Owners of older properties may opt to have a water meter. This will mean that you pay for what water you use and this will include garden watering.

Hosepipe bans and drought orders

The regional authorities that administer water are able, under times of restriction, to

WHAT'S NEW

During 2007 DEFRA reassessed the existing regulations and recommended a more flexible approach to restrictions on water usage. Future bans are likely to include the filling of swimming pools, hot tubs and fountains, and cleaning of patios. Garden irrigation will be restricted in commercial and public gardens as well as private, but there will be flexibility where there is a recognized significant plant collection. It is not clear as yet as to whether gardeners will be allowed to use microbore and drip irrigation systems.

impose a hosepipe ban. This means that gardeners are not allowed to use hosepipes to water their gardens in any way. You can use as much water as you like if you use a watering can, although you cannot fill this from a hosepipe, only from the tap. Strangely allotments are not covered by this legislation and may be watered during a ban. Any sort of irrigation system, however efficient, is covered by the ban and may not be used. By contrast owners of swimming pools are allowed to refill them. You may also refill garden pools containing fish, or wash down your patio but you may not clean your car.

Drought orders are much more restrictive and generally only imposed where there is a severe shortage of water that has built up over a number of dry years. Such measures are likely to extend a watering ban to allotments, public parks and sports grounds. It will also restrict the filling of swimming pools and the washing of cars and other commercial cleaning. Under very severe drought, the water supply to houses could be terminated and water be supplied only to areas by means of stand-pipes in the roads.

Alternative water supplies

Responsible gardeners who wish to water areas of their gardens will need to explore alternative sources of water that do not deplete domestic water reserves. This may become essential where mains water is restricted for garden use or quite simply highly desirable due to cost. This will usually be the case where water metering is in place and water is charged by usage. Some of the alternatives are more environmentally acceptable than others.

Water storage & recycling

The most simple means of water storage is by way of a water butt. These traditional containers are positioned underneath the outlets from the downpipes from roof gutters. This will provide a basic but small store of water, usually no more than 200 litres at a time. Based on average UK annual rainfall and the size of an average roof, the potential for collecting rainwater increases to a massive 72,000 litres per annum. In practical terms this means much larger tanks or a series of water butts are needed to make particular use of this free resource. This has been based on high winter rainfall but in

BELOW A simple domestic water butt such as this one will retain sufficient rainwater to maintain containers and small areas during a short dry spell.

these times of climate change, this may not always be so.

Some water authorities offer special deals on water butts and diverter kits to channel water from downpipes to the butt. One DIY chain offers large vertical tanks moulded to look like classical columns, terracotta pithoi and oak barrels – all made from plastic. Now whilst the aesthetics of these might not fit in with everyone's idea of garden style, if they encourage more gardeners to store water then they are a success.

Larger tanks, either above or underground, are of course possible and any serious gardener may well consider making a long-term investment in such a facility. This can be used for storage of large quantities of rain-water collected during the winter. One partic-ular and more extensive system works by means of a series of large columns that sit tight against the side of the house and extend to the gutter line. They collect rainwater direct from the roof gutters, which can then be distributed, purely by means of the force of gravity. For faster and more efficient distribu-tion of your stored water, you may want to consider the use of a pump. At least one irriga-tion company offers a special water butt pump. It is submersible, totally self-contained and has an integral easy-clean filter which prevents damage from dirty water.

Undergrounds tanks for garden use are a more serious installation and will require excava-tion of a sizeable hole, with all the problems of access for digging equipment and disposal of all the surplus excavated soil. In some areas you may also need to inform the local authorities. The system will need to include simple filtration, vermin traps, an overflow and a pump that takes the water from the top of the tank and avoids

any settled sediment. This will be a serious and costly investment.

Such rainwater is a good source of water for most garden purposes. It is particularly good for ericaceous plants that will tolerate water with a high pH, which is often so with tap water. Stored rainwater is not good for small seedlings or use in a greenhouse as it will usually be infected with plant pathogens and is likely to cause damping-off and other diseases in young or delicate plants. Water butts should be covered to prevent the growth of algae, which turns the water green in the presence of sunlight. A commercial additive is available to keep the water in a water butt clean and algae free.

Recycled water

When we get to the realms of large storage tanks, it is well worth considering the use of 'grey' water for garden purposes. This is the recycling of used water from household areas such as baths, showers, washing machines and dishwashers. In general it is thought that most detergents are harmless to plants, although if you are considering using grey water for gardens it is best to combine this with eco-friendly household products.

Obviously as well as a storage tank, modi-fications will need to be made to plumbing systems to divert waste water to the storage tanks. On a short-term basis grey water can be siphoned straight from a bath via a hosepipe and used directly on the garden, although this is rather fiddly and really only a stop-gap approach. Such sources of water also have the advantage that they are continually being produced throughout the year so that storage tanks required will be smaller than those where reliance is on rainwater only.

You might well wonder about the risk of Legionella with such systems. With the water stored underground where it is dark cool and is kept well oxygenated. Legionella cannot develop in these conditions. Also Legionella is transmitted by means of a fine vapour that is inhaled so providing you do not use stored water for systems such as mist units, there is no risk.

In large gardens a pond can be used for storage of winter rainfall and subsequent use in summer. It must be realized though that such a facility will be subject to evaporation and the resource you are trying to conserve may rapidly dwindle in hot weather before you even start to use it. Deep ponds with a limited surface area are best used as a reservoir. A suitable pump will need to be used to distribute the water and an adequate filter to avoid the whole system being blocked by debris and other material that will inevitably collect in an open area of water. Such pools may be so designed that they are an integral part of the design of the garden, but remember if you add aquatic plants and fish there may be a conflict when you start to drain the water during a summer drought. Such pools are better regarded as simple reflecting pools possibly with fountains rather than complete ecosystems.

Later on we shall be talking about irriga-tion systems and emphasizing that some narrow bore systems are the best for economic water usage. However these may not be the most suitable where stored or grey water is used. Inevitably such water will contain some particles left over from its prefious use and unless it is thoroughly filtered, these will block any irrigation system with small tubes or delicate orifices.

Boreholes and bowsers

If you have a large garden and a budget to match, it is possible to have your own borehole drilled and become self-sufficient with your own water supply. It is an expensive exercise though and debatable as to whether this is environmentally friendly as you will still be drawing from the underground aquifers that feed our commercial water supplies.

Initially you will need a hydro geological survey to predict whether there is a suitable pocket of underground water that can be sourced. Sometimes a trial borehole will be drilled before the main borehole, in order to ascertain exactly where the water is and its quality. In some areas drilling may have to be very deep and costs will make this non-economical. Depending on the amounts you may wish to extract, you may need to get an abstraction license. In some countries this is only needed if you use more than 20m^3 per day, which is a lot of water in private garden terms. A powerful pump will also be need to draw water up from the depths and distribute it around your garden. This, in turn, will be using fuel, which again brings in questionable green ethics.

However after the initial costs of drilling and equipping, in theory you have free water, which can be used for the garden and other non-drinking purposes. In some areas the water may be totally pure and as good as some bottled spring waters.

During the recent drought in the UK some keen and wealthy gardeners found that a loophole to legislation, whereby it was possible to buy a commercial tanker or bowser of water and use this to irrigate their gardens. A very expensive and non-environmentally friendly answer.

SECTION TWO
The Practicalities

Soils and water conservation

Soil is the very basis from which gardens grow. It is uniquely important but also often misunderstood and neglected. Soil provides anchorage for plants and is their essential source of nutrition, air and water – all vital for a plants survival. While this book concentrates on water issues, a basic understanding of soils and their improvement is one of the keys to achieving a successful and attractive garden.

Know your soil

Gardeners often speak of topsoil, which is the rich, well cultivated uppermost layer of soil in which most plant roots grow and therefore where moisture is critical. This is generally around 30 cm (12 in) deep, although it may vary considerably according whether it has been well cultivated or neglected. Subsoil is the material below topsoil, which is generally poorer, more compacted and less rich. By cultivating soil deeply and adding soil improvers, the depth of topsoil in a garden can be increased. This in turn will result in increased root growth and access to additional water, resulting in good plant growth.

Soils are made up of solids, liquids and air, and the proportions of these are critical. A good soil will have 50–60 per cent mineral solids, about 5 per cent organic matter and 35–45 per cent air and water. The space for air and water is very important and when a soil is compacted, say with heavy wear or vehicles driving over it, the spaces for air and water are squashed out. This makes it much more difficult for plants to grow adequately. Correct cultivation opens up a soil for air and water to penetrate.

We have spoken earlier about water in the soil and the components of most soils, sand, silt and clay. When we speak of these we are describing a soil's texture.

You can determine the type of soil you have by rubbing a small sample between your wetted fingers. A sandy soil is easy to ascertain as the sample feels rough and gritty and does not stick together. A clay soil will feel sticky and a larger sample of it will roll into a shiny ball. Silty soils are more difficult to determine by this test but generally feel silky and smooth. With a loam you may be able to feel all the constituents in the mixture. Depending on the proportions, we may speak about having a sandy loam if the proportion of sand is high or a clay loam at the other end of the scale and so on. It is useful to understand this in order to know how best to treat the soils you are cultivating.

RIGHT *Alliums* and *Eschscholtzias* provide a mass of early summer colour in this dry garden at Hyde Hall in rain starved East Anglia, UK.

Sandy Soils

These are generally free draining, easy to cultivate and tend to warm up quickly in the spring, making them good for vegetable production. In particular root crops will grow well. They do not retain water well, so dry out quickly. They tend to need more irrigation in the summer and are also often poor soils needing more nutrients added regularly.

Clay Soils

Clay-based soils are heavy, generally difficult to cultivate and regarded as more of a challenge. They can be wet, poorly drained and therefore often slow to warm up in the spring. They do however retain more moisture through the summer and are generally regarded as rich soils. They are good for fruit and permanent plants such as roses.

Silty Soils

This type of soil is not so common, although does occur in certain areas and in particular near to rivers. These soils generally behave more like sandy soils but are richer and less prone to drying out. They are also good soils for growing vegetables.

Improving soils

One of the most important ways of improving a soil and increasing its ability to hold water is by adding organic matter. Most soils will contain some from the natural processes of death and decay of everything that lives in the soil, but it is nearly always worth adding extra. Organic matter is made of very fine particles that hold large quantities of water in the soil – like the sponge we discussed on page 20.

There are many different sources of organic matter but they will all be originally derived from living materials, either plant or animal in origin. Organic materials can be incorporated into the soil when new areas are prepared or spread on the surface as a mulch. In this case worms and other creatures will incorporate into the soil over a period of time.

Composting

Because organic matter is so important and composting such a valuable process, we will spend some time looking at this in detail. A compost heap provides a means of disposing of the majority of our garden waste and some of our kitchen waste, without having to send it to a land-fill site. The end product is then a valuable commodity for enriching the soil and

SOURCES OF ORGANIC MATTER
- Garden compost
- Recycled green waste (from your local authority)
- Farmyard manure
- Chicken manure
- Spent mushroom compost
- Leafmould
- Composted seaweed
- Composted bracken
- Spent hops or brewer's grains (from a brewery)

All of these can be valuable and may vary in price according to whether there is a local source. Farmyard or chicken manure must be well rotted before use or it can damage the roots of plants. Mushroom compost is good but is quite often alkaline and so should never be used with plants which need an acid soil. Your own garden compost is one of the best and cheapest sources so it is well worth while running a good compost heap.

increasing water retention. A compost heap needs no more space than about 1 square metre/yard, although it's better to have two and bigger gardens will need a bigger heap to deal with all the waste. To keep it tidy, a compost heap can be made within a bin of some sort. Proprietary bins made of plastic are available from garden centres or in some areas free from your local authority. Alternatively a very usable bin can be made from old wooden pallets. Three will form a suitable enclosure. The fourth side needs to be loose so that access to the heap is possible.

Many different types of waste can be used in a compost heap. Some rough loose material is useful at the bottom to keep the heap well drained. If you had a previous heap, there are usually some tough remains that may not have been rotted properly and will be a useful base for the next one. A good heap is made up of a mixture of materials. Some wastes such as hedge clippings can be quite woody whereas others like grass mowings are very soft and lush. Mixing the various materials together helps them to decompose. Small domestic shredders are now readily available and make it possible to process woody material such as prunings or tough hedge trimmings into smaller components that will decompose more evenly and quickly.

A compost heap will be constructed as materials are available but ideally different

MATERIALS TO ADD TO A COMPOST HEAP

- Weeds (not perennial weeds)
- Grass mowings
- Autumn leaves
- Dead plants and crops
- Dead flower heads or cut flowers
- Rootballs or used potting compost
- Vegetable peelings from the kitchen
- Tea leaves and coffee grounds
- Torn up newspaper
- Animal manures (such as pet's bedding)
- Hedge trimmings (chopped or shredded)
- Prunings (if shredded)

Avoid perennial weeds, diseased plants and cooked foods or meats, which will attract vermin.

RIGHT Composting is basic good gardening and the resulting organic matter is of great value in helping soils retain moisture.

types of materials should be mixed as added. If the constituents are dry, water should be added, or decomposition will not take place if it is dry. Compost activators are available, which can be added to encourage the natural organisms to work, but these are not usually necessary if the heap is a good mixture of different ingredients.

About six weeks after the heap has been completed, it is a good practice to 'turn' the heap. This means taking the half-formed compost out, mixing it up, letting fresh air into the heap and stacking up again for the process to complete. Where there is space, this is where a second bin comes in handy. The compost can be forked out of one bin, shaken up and re-stacked in the next one. This process is not essential but certainly helps in producing good compost in a short space of time. A foul smell from a compost heap usually means that it is too wet, often from too many lush materials such as wet grass mowings. Shaking it out and adding drier materials will usually help to get it back on course.

Compost is ready when it resembles a crumbly dark brown material in which you can barely recognise the original constituents. It should smell earthy but not unpleasant. This may take between three to six months depending on the time of year.

Drainage

This may seem an odd subject to be found in a book that is primarily dealing with water shortage and growing plants under drought conditions. However global warming has brought us a number of extremes and as well as excessively dry weather, we also often experience very wet spells in winter and our plants and gardens must be able to cope with this as well.

Many of the plants that are recommended for survival under drought conditions just will not tolerate winter waterlogging. This brings us back to good soil preparation and ensuring that there is a good deep loose soil profile. Excess water must be able to drain away easily and quickly. It may be beneficial with some plants to add extra sand or grit at planting time to aid drainage. It sounds like a contradiction but what many plants require is a well drained but water retentive soil. This is achieved by plenty of organic matter and good cultivation.

It is also paradoxical that plants growing in waterlogged conditions are more likely to suffer from drought. Quite simply, plants growing in a waterlogged soil will have a limited and shallow root system as the waterlogged conditions will have killed some of the roots. A plant with a restricted root system will not respond as well when the soil dries out as a plant with a healthier and deeper root system. Also any plant that has had part of its root system destroyed by waterlogging is likely to have been invaded by root rotting fungi and such a plant will be weakened and less likely to withstand other adverse conditions.

Simple improvements can be made to drainage by good deep cultivation. There is often a hard impenetrable layer in many soils just under the topsoil. Breaking this up by double digging will help to improve drainage and root run. Adding sharp sand and grit to a badly drained soil will also help to keep the pore spaces open and aid the free flow of excess water away from the surface. In a really waterlogged situation, you may have to consider installing a system of underground piped drainage. This is best done by professionals who can achieve the correct falls on a drain and will also know where to find an outlet for the drainage water. Most urban gardens don't have a convenient ditch. A simpler solution to this is to dig a trench and partially fill with loose stone or gravel. Cover with a horticultural membrane and then refill with the topsoil. This will help channel excess water away from the surface but again should ideally be directed to a place where it can freely flow away.

Mulching

This is hardly the sexiest activity in the gardening textbook but it is something that all waterwise gardeners need to be really passionate about. It is key to water conservation. Mulching is a traditional technique that has been used in gardens for many years but has become of particular importance since we have needed to concentrate on water conservation.

Mulching is simply the addition of a thick layer of additional material over the surface of the soil. This acts in a number of ways to improve plant growth and also reduce garden maintenance. A good deep mulch reduces the

BELOW This simple grass and gravel garden has a dramatic appearance, with very low maintenance, and the planted areas just drift into the pathways.

loss of water from the soil by evaporation, which is our key reason for considering it here. You can check out the value of this for yourself by applying a mulch to parts of the garden in winter or spring when the soil is moist. Leave some similar areas uncovered. Go back to them in summer when the soil has started to dry out and check the soil under the mulch. You will undoubtedly find that there is moisture there when exposed soil is looking and feeling dry.

Mulching also reduces soil temperature, which will in turn also reduce water loss. In addition mulches will prevent most weed seeds germinating and this will reduce the competition that weeds make for soil moisture. Overall it's got to be good for plants. Finally most mulches quite simply look good and provide an attractive setting for plants.

Mulching can be used in almost any part of the garden and for most plants but it is of particular importance for establishing new plantings and for plants that are very sensitive to water loss.

Organic Mulches

These are a whole host of various materials that have originated from living sources. In most cases they are similar to the organic soil improvers we have spoken about but the materials we shall focus on here are long lasting and break down slowly. They have an extra benefit in that they break down and release nutrients into the soil and therefore aid plant nutrition. The disadvantage of this breakdown process is that your mulch is constantly shrinking and will need to be topped up, often on an annual basis.

Generally, mulches with larger particles act most effectively. A finely ground mulch will

tend to act like the soil itself and draw up moisture to the surface by capillarity where it will evaporate. With a coarse chunky mulch, the pore spaces are far too large for this and the mulch stays dry on the surface, whilst the soil remains moist beneath.

BARK has become popular in recent years, particularly for mulching commercial land-scapes. It is a by-product from the timber industry. There are a number of different grades, from smaller milled, evenly sized crumbs through to big chunky nuggets, both of which are effective. Some suppliers also offer bark that has been tinted with coloured dyes. It's all a matter of opinion but to my mind, they certainly don't look natural and the colours are not intense enough to make a statement. Some of the cheaper bark products are mixed with wood chips and, although this is not a major problem, you should ensure that you are not paying too much for an inferior product. Beware of anything that is described as 'all purpose amenity mulch'.

WOOD CHIPS are a cheaper by-product both from the timber industry and from tree surgery works. Arborists produce vast quantities from their prunings and they are always available. They are not quite as attractive as bark due to their lighter colour, although they are almost as effective as a mulch. They do however have a negative effect on the soil that needs to be considered. As woodchips break down they take nitrogen, one of the main plant nutrients, from the soil. Therefore a mulch of woodchips can have the effect of considerably slowing plant growth. They should never be incorporated into the soil for this reason – just left on the surface as a mulch. To avoid the starvation problem, you need to remember to add an extra dose of a nitrogenous fertiliser when using woodchips.

There is also the slight risk that woodchips may carry a disease called honey fungus if they have been produced from an infected tree. Fresh woodchips are also inclined to heat up in large quantities so they should really be matured before using. Woodchips should always be allowed to mature and cool before using as a mulch. If used fresh, there is always a risk that a good thick mulch may heat up and 'cook' the plant, resulting in scorch around its neck.

LEAFMOULD is a natural product produced as leaves from deciduous trees rot down. It takes at least a year to produce and will by then be a dark sweet smelling material. Anyone who has lots of trees will be able to produce this easily from gathered leaves. There are also always surplus leaves in your area, in the roads and other people's gardens. Some leaves make better leafmould than others. Oak and beech are good and horse chestnut is slow to rot but a good mixture will decompose down success-fully. Leafmould makes an effective and attractive mulch but tends to be short-lived and disappears within a season.

MANURES such as farmyard, stable or chicken manures can be useful and they will probably be quite rich and feed plants as well, so are good for mulching plants such as roses and fruit bushes which need high fertilizer regimes. The duration of such products will also depend on what bedding has been used for the animals, as this will obviously be part of the end product. Straw and sawdust are common bedding materials. Sawdust will be the slowest to break down and therefore provide the

longest lasting mulch. All animal manures must be partially composted before they are used on planted areas or scorch may occur from the high levels of ammonia and other chemicals within the material.

GARDEN COMPOST made from your own garden waste is quite acceptable but like leaf-mould will probably be short lasting. Garden compost can also have problems of harbouring and spreading weed seeds unless it has been very well produced. A carefully made compost heap will heat up and sterilize the product but poorly made compost will not and as soon as it is spread on the surface, weeds will start to germinate.

PINE NEEDLES may occasionally be available and these make a very attractive, unusual mulch that is both effective and long lasting. If gathered with some pine cones it is doubly attractive. You should not collect this or leaf-mould from a forest or woodland without the owner's permission.

STRAW is readily and cheaply available, although it is not a very effective mulch as it tends to be too open. Its use has traditionally been in strawberry production, where it acts rather more in keeping the fruit off the ground than as an effective mulch. It is slow to break down and as it does it removes the nitrogen from the soil. If used for strawberries, it will usually need to be raked up at the end of the season and composted.

A recent commercial product is available that consists of partially composted wheat straw. This has a dark earthy brown colour and is chopped to give usable particles. It is claimed that it will last for one to two season

but like all organic materials is broken down and absorbed into the soil.

COCOA SHELLS are a by-product from the chocolate industry and are marketed as a mulching material. It is said that they provide an effective mulch with only a thin 2.5 cm (1 in) layer. Cocoa shells tends to grow a white mould in damp warm weather when they are first laid but this soon disappears. When new they exudes a strong chocolaety smell that some people may find attractive. There is however some documented risk to dogs that have become attracted to the smell, eaten the mulch and been poisoned by the high theobromine levels within it. If you have pets it may be advisable to avoid this product or at least use with caution.

Applying mulches

Generally the thicker a mulch can be applied, the more effective and longer lasting it will be. Most materials should be applied at between 5 cm (2 in) and 10 cm (4 in) A good average for bark, wood chippings, pine needles and compost would be 7.5 cm (3 in). Some fine materials such as fine graded bark, leafmould and cocoa shells are effective used in thinner layers. With a thick mulch one would need also to ensure that the crowns of herbaceous plants and crops such as strawberries are not smothered. Top up mulches when they start to deteriorate and before the soil can be seen between the particles. By that stage they are no longer effective at either water conservation or weed control.

LEFT (Clockwise from top left) Cobbles provide an attractive mulch but need a membrane underneath. Gravel is available in many colours. Wood chippings and bark are well known for their value as a mulch. Coloured glass is a recent addition to the materials available to use as a mulch.

ONE TO AVOID
Grass mowings do not make a good mulch, even if you do have a ready supply. They contain a high proportion of nitrogen and water and are unlikely to break down naturally in or on the soil on their own. Generally when spread on the surface they make a nasty tight cap to the soil, which prevents air and any rain from entering. They are likely to be unsightly and undoubtedly smelly – not the thing to mix with your roses! Grass mowings are best mixed into a compost heap and do very well to balance other more woody materials such as chopped hedge trimmings.

Inorganic mulches (described below) these can be applied as much thinner layers, around 2.5 cm (1 in) thick. This is usually quite adequate, particularly as most of them will be used as a topping over a sheet membrane of some sort.

Mulches should be applied to weed-free soils in the early months of the year whilst the soil is still naturally moist. Don't apply to a frozen soil as the mulch will tend to insulate and keep the soil colder for longer than necessary. The material should be barrowed onto the site and tipped in small piles between plants. It may even be easier to distribute it using a bucket. The material is then spread out evenly. A garden fork is probably the easiest tool for this but in some situations a rake may be useful. Tease it round and under the plants so that all the soil is covered. Any shoots, leaves or plants that have become buried should be 'tickled' out with the fork so that they are not smothered.

Although in general, mulches are highly beneficial, they do have a few disadvantages.

AVOVE With choice moisture loving plants, such as Hostas, spread a generous mulch of bark or wood chippings over the whole rootzone.

Birds are attracted to mulches and will inevitably pick them over to see what food materials they can find hiding amongst the mulch and throw them all over the place. Also, when applied on any slope or if the soil is higher than the surrounding edges of the bed, the mulch will inevitably find its way over the edge and onto surrounding surfaces so will have to be swept back into place every so often. There is also a risk of fire.

Inorganic Mulches

Here we have a range of generally inert materials, some derived from natural materials such as rocks and in other cases from synthetic or recycled products. Being inorganic, they will have little reaction with soil organisms and will not decay. This means virtually all will be long lasting and therefore require very little if any topping up. There tends to be a far greater palette of colours and effects with inorganic mulches and so they can be used to create attractive foils for the plants being mulched. For example, silver foliage plants can be mulched with black stone chippings or golden junipers with blue glass nuggets for striking designs.

NATURAL STONE PRODUCTS are undoubtedly the commonest of the inorganic mulches. Gravel itself has given rise to a specific style of gardening of its own, which we shall discuss later. Although most garden centres tend to sell these materials, they will often be at high prices in small bags. For an extensive

FIRE PREVENTION

One of the minor but annoying risks with organic mulches is that they can be a fire hazard. A casually thrown cigarette butt landing on bone dry bark mulch can turn into a small fire. This usually smoulders and smokes rather than flaring up but the risk is there nevertheless and such small fires could pass to more flammable materials. Every year there are disastrous fires in areas experiencing drought and they are often started from a casually thrown cigarette butt and no one wants their garden as the epicentre of a major fire!

For this reason one does need to be careful with mulched areas near to buildings and especially timber constructions. As an alternative you could use one of the inorganic mulches described below for areas near buildings or you could zone areas near the house for moisture requiring plants, which are therefore given some water. Great care should obviously be exercised with disposal of cigarettes or with any outdoor sources of fire such as barbeques.

Some plants are more inflammable than others. Anything which has an oily or resinous wood such as pines, junipers or rosemary is likely to be flammable. Keep these away from buildings and also anything which discards a lot of debris such as pine needles which would dry and become a fire hazard. Close to buildings use succulent plants which because of their high water content are less likely to burn, These would include species such as *Sedum*, *Yucca*, *Phormium*, *Lampranthus* and *Agave*.

project and for some more unusual materials look for a local supplier of landscape materials. A whole range of different products will be available and available in plastic bags or by

the tonne. Prices vary considerably and something unusual like a polished black gravel will be expensive.

SEA SHELLS would be a possibility for a specific garden area. Mussels, cockles and oyster shells are commercially available but the cost is high. If you collect them yourself I would suggest washing before using in the garden to remove excess salt. Remember that a high proportion of the material of seas shells is calcareous so they are likely to raise soil pH and be unsuitable for use around acid-loving plants. Take care if you collect them yourself. In some areas it is illegal to remove stones and shells from coastal areas.

TUMBLED GLASS is recycled glass that has been crushed and then tumbled to remove sharp edges. It is usually available in a number of colours such as blue, green, white, brown and sometimes other colours such as plum or black. Because of the brighter colours it is wise to use this in small areas or as a statement rather than as a general mulch. As this is made from a recycled product it is very environmentally friendly. Ultimately glass will break down into silica, the very natural sand material from which it was originally made.

CRUSHED BRICK is another eco-friendly material as once again it is recycled. Many demolition firms now recycle a large proportion of the construction materials. Broken red bricks are crushed and make a distinct attractively coloured mulch. It gives the effect of red volcanic rock which is generally not widely available. Be sure to get a material that has had the dust and fines removed.

Stone mulches

GRAVEL AND STONE CHIPPINGS are available in a host of different colours and sizes, from fine up to quite large pebbles. Different colours are available from golden yellows and browns to almost blue and green. Some expensive types may be available such as white marble or black quartz chips. Some chippings can be angular while others may be rounded and shiny. However some startling effects can be obtained with these materials. Stone mulches are quite durable and can be used as path surfacing materials so that the planted and mulched areas blend into walkways.

PEBBLES are natural aggregates from quarries or from beaches and come in many different colours and sizes. Barleycorn quartz is particularly unusual with a mix of soft cream and peach shades. Some are selected as flat pebbles and give another effect. The green and peach shades are especially attractive.

CRUSHED AGGREGATES are made, as the name suggests, by crushing larger stone and then grading it to certain sizes. Again an amazing array of types are available. As well as all the normal neutral stone colours, there are red porphyry, a lovely terracotta colour, black basalt, white marble and pink granite, to mention but a few.

LEFT This uncomplicated design makes use of a gravel surface and drought tolerant ivy to give a quiet but green oasis in this public garden.

SLATE CHIPPINGS are flat and can be available in greys, pale blues, plum or greenish tints. Several different sizes are available enabling different effects. Although they can sometimes look drab and dusty, a light shower of rain or dew will bring back the colours instantly. Paddlestones are larger flat pieces of slate.

COBBLES are really just large round stones, typically 5 cm (2 in) or more. Several natural colours are available as well as Scottish beach cobbles which are a lovely mix of colours. There are classy grey and white streaked ones, known as Angel stones, and some rather pricey colour selected cobbles in blacks, reds, dark greens and gold. They can be used as a mulch directly around larger plants, although they tend not to be effective on their own as the spaces between them are too large. They are best used over a membrane of some sort, which really acts as the mulch, with the cobbles merely the aesthetic finish. However they will have some value in keeping the soil insulated and cool. Mix them with smaller stones to get the best overall effect.

FLINTS are like large black glassy cobbles and usually have a white outer coating as they occur naturally in chalk. Usually most flints show an interesting mix of black and white. Knapped flints are split and are a traditional building material. In some areas flint rejects may be available cheap for landscaping.

RUBBER MULCHES are manufactured from recycled tyres and processed into crumbs. Sometimes these may be coloured. They are long lasting and, as they are recycled, have some ecological value. However rubber mulches lack the aesthetic appeal of other mulches and it's unlikely that they will ever be viewed as attractive enough for anything other than large scale commercial land-scapes. Also the appropriateness of contaminating the soil with something such as rubber that may never decompose is also questionable.

BELOW A mulch mat such as this one will help to retain the moisture in the soil around the roots of a young tree and also prevent weed growth.

SHEET MULCHES include all the various different types of sheet material including polythene, permeable woven membranes and recycled materials such as old carpets and newspapers. Most of these are unsightly but very effective and will either be relegated to utilitarian areas, such as the vegetable garden, or be covered with another material such as gravel.

Black polythene makes an excellent mulch for the vegetable garden and plants such as strawberries can be very successfully grown in it. The sheets should be laid down first and anchored with wire pins or the edges dug into a slit trench. When planting, make a cross slit for each plant and plant through the polythene

ensuring that the minimum soil is left exposed. Remember that polythene will not let the water through so when you are covering large areas, some slits should be made to allow the water in.

There are various proprietary types of woven polypropylene or woven fibre membranes that are manufactured specifically for horticulture. They have the advantage of being permeable enough to let water through but tough enough to prevent weeds emerging. They are often used underneath gravel mulches and have the added advantage of preventing the gravel mixing with the soil, which inevitably happens over a period of time. Again we normally plant through them.

There is also a bio-degradable paper mulch that is available for use in vegetable production. It comes in sheet form through which you can plant. Being white it has the advantage of reflecting light and therefore keeping the soil cooler in hot weather. At the end of the season it can be dug in or mixed into the compost heap.

MULCH MATS are available as individual round or square sections made of various materials that can be used around individual trees. Some are made of mixtures of biodegradable materials such as jute, wood fibre or recycled wool to ensure that after they have served their purpose in mulching a young tree, they will rot back into the soil and disappear. They will usually require anchoring down with pins or with a layer of another mulch material on top.

Water retaining polymers

In recent years various artificial products have been developed that can be added to soils to help retain the water. Most are based on the synthetic polymer polyacrylamide. This is supplied as dry crystals which are mixed with the soil or potting compost. The soil is then thoroughly moistened before planting takes place. The crystals swell to a jelly-like material very much like thick wallpaper paste in appearance. The water contained within the gel is available to plants as they grow. They also have the ability to hold nutrients which might otherwise be washed out of the soil. These are then available for plant growth.

These products should only ever be used at the correct rate and because of their costs are only really practical in small areas. Manufacturers' claims suggest that these products can increase the water holding capacity of soils by 300–800 per cent. Their greatest use is in containers and hanging baskets, which are particularly likely to dry out quickly.

Water retaining polymers can also be useful with the establishment of new and valuable plants such as freshly planted trees. Ultimately they are biodegradable so will disappear into the soil. Sometimes you may also have a plant amongst a general planting, such as a Hosta, which requires more water than its neighbours. Incorporating some granules into the soil around it will help to give it the conditions it requires without additional special watering.

Some manufacturers offer small mats that are impregnated with water retaining granules and these can be used to line a hanging basket or planter. These are supplied dry as large round or square pellets, which swell when moistened. They are useful because they not only reduce the need for general watering but they will hold enough water for one to two weeks, providing a good holiday watering solution.

Cultural issues

Many of our gardening techniques are based on tradition and practices that have been tried and tested over the years. With the advent of global warming and the changes to the patterns of weather, we are having to rethink and amend a number of these. One of the most obvious to all gardeners is the way in which grass seems now to grow for a much longer period of the year. We have barely put the mower away in late autumn before the grass is growing again and needs a winter cut.

Planting issues

In recent years a high proportion of plants have been grown and supplied in containers. These can be planted throughout the year with a high rate of success. However summer planting has always been dependent on the ability to regularly water freshly planted areas until the new plants have developed a thorough new root system. With the typical wet summers of the past, even this has not always been necessary. Now as we are experiencing shortages of water, summer planting and irrigation becomes less feasible.

If you are planting a new garden in a low water area, try to plant in the autumn or winter. This is a return to the traditional and more conservative approach from the past. Many plants including trees and shrubs will grow new roots during the dormant winter months without any sign of top growth. This means that when the warmer weather of spring arrives, the roots are ahead of the shoot growth and able to easily supply the new growth. Such a well balanced plant will be more able to withstand water shortage later in the season.

Preparation

The old adage 'a penny for the plant and a pound for the hole' has always been true. The more time and effort you spend on careful planting, the more likely it is that establishment and growth is going to be successful. It is every bit as true when planting in areas of water shortage. Make sure that the soil is carefully prepared with plenty of organic matter and that the soil is thoroughly loosened, breaking up any areas of compacted soil so that roots can penetrate deeply. This is very important. Plants that are relying on moisture from just the surface layers of soils will dry out quickly and show signs of stress. Those that have deep root systems will be able to survive longer and tap into sources of water that are unavailable to shallow rooted plants.

We should always try to avoid damage to roots when we are planting but this is particularly true when planting in the waterwise garden, where rapid establishment and the

RIGHT Prairie plantings, like this one at Pensthorpe in Norfolk, England, show how much colour is possible with a careful choice of suitable plants despite low water .

development of a strong root system is essential. Handle plants carefully to avoid breaking roots and if you have plants such as trees or rose bushes with bare, exposed roots, always be sure to keep them covered to avoid desiccating. Dry roots become dead roots very rapidly. It always worth ensuring that roots are moist before planting. A container-grown plant should have its rootball watered and an open ground plant should have its roots dipped in water for a few minutes before planting.

If you are planting from a container and the roots are particularly congested, it is often advisable to loosen these but do so carefully so that they unravel with minimum breakages. This is particularly recommended if you are planting in the autumn when the plant will have plenty of time to re-establish. Be more cautious if you are spring planting.

Aftercare

Where you have plants with a lot of top growth and very few roots, it will help in the establishment if the top is pruned to bring this back more into balance. Otherwise when growth starts there will be insufficient roots to draw water for the rest of the plant. Many young trees, fruit bushes and roses will benefit from this even though they may be dormant and not showing leaves.

Some leafy plants will respond well to similar treatment. For example, if we are dividing flag irises in mid summer it is normal to trim the top growth by about half to leave just a short fan of leaves. Likewise if you are transplanting leeks in midsummer it is best to trim the tops by about 50 per cent before planting.

It may seem surprising but young and small plants usually transplant and establish more easily than older bigger plants. This is particularly so with trees. Should you wish to plant a windbreak or a small copse and not want to constantly water it, then use small young saplings and mulch mats. Such small trees will usually grow rapidly with a minimum of extra attention.

Transplanting evergreens can be tricky as they have leaves at all seasons and will therefore be losing moisture by transpiration throughout the year. The best time for transplanting evergreens is early to mid autumn or again in mid spring. At these times roots re-establish very quickly. If you feel that there is a likelihood that they will not re-establish easily, it is worth giving them some extra attention. You can protect individual plants with a temporary screen to reduce the sunshine and water loss. This would ideally be with a quick 'shroud' made from horticultural fleece wrapped around a wigwam of canes or even polythene, although this on its own is inclined to sweat. You can also use anti-transpirant spray, which is a harmless plastic type compound which can be sprayed on foliage to stops it losing excess water. This is manufactured primarily for Christmas trees to stop them dropping their needles in the warmth of a house but works just as well on other plants outside.

Choosing your plants

The later chapters of this book will look in more detail at suitable plants for dry climates, but at this stage I want to emphasize how important it is to choose the right plants. So many of us, myself included, often make impulse purchases of plants that attract us. When we get home we often don't know where to position them or what conditions they like.

The result is often disappointment when they fail to thrive.

When planning a waterwise garden we need to choose plants that will grow and thrive in the situations we have. So many people try to fight the conditions in their gardens by choosing unsuitable plants. If you have an acid soil and a shady garden, then plants that like acid conditions and low light levels are the likely plants to thrive. Not surprising really – choose them, buy them and grow them. Often gardens will have different microclimates and given time we will discover these and find we have special conditions that enable us to grow certain plants. Work with the conditions and not against them. It may be stating the obvious but as gardeners we often fail to observe that basic premise.

Windbreaks, shade and shelter

We have already observed that plants lose more water by transpiration when conditions are windy so it is important to ensure that plants in the waterwise garden do not suffer from excess exposure to wind. For those of us that live in small enclosed town gardens this may be irrelevant, but some of you may garden in exposed coastal areas, or country regions where the wind blows. All exposed gardens should be sheltered with a windbreak of tough trees and shrubs that will filter the wind and reduce its speed. Hedges and permeable fencing such as wattle hurdles will have a similar effect but brick walls and close-boarded fencing do not. These merely cause turbulence with the wind hitting the wall and tumbling over in all sorts of eddies and currents that damage plants.

A garden that is totally exposed with no shade from trees or other buildings is also likely to be exceedingly hot in the full summer sun. Some shade is always valuable in reducing temperatures and enabling you to grow a wider range of plantss.

BELOW A good strong hedge will provide valuable shelter in exposed areas, enabling more tender plants to be established, and reduce water loss.

WINDBREAK PLANTS

Good plants for acting as a windbreak will be a combination of trees and shrubs that are generally fast growing and very tough. The best windbreaks are not necessarily the densest plants as a good windbreak will filter the wind slowing it down and reducing its force. A mix of evergreens and deciduous plants is best, with some trees and shrubs to fill in the gaps at low level. It is also useful to include species such as *Tamarix* for fast growth and immediate impact with longer lasting species such as *Quercus* for permanency. The following are some good toughies suitable for windbreaks in dry areas.

Berberis stenophylla
Cotoneaster simonsii
Euonymus europaeus
Hippophae rhamnoides
Olearia traversii
Pinus nigra var. *maritima*
Prunus laurocerasus
Quercus ilex
Tamarix tetrandra

In very exposed areas it may be useful to use a plastic mesh or wattle hurdles to give a newly planted windbreak a chance to establish. Don't be tempted to use a solid fence as this, like brick walls, will not filter the wind but just cause turbulence as the wind cannot pass through.

Some of the plants that I will suggest for a waterwise garden are on the borderlines of hardiness, coming from Mediterranean areas. Windbreaks and shade trees also give a level of shelter and create slightly warmer conditions that will be beneficial to such plants.

Pests and diseases

Sadly gardens are never without their problems, and there are other creatures within your garden that will be enjoying your plants as well as you. Pests and diseases will appear in even the best maintained gardens. Any attack from pathogens will spoil the appearance of plants and weaken their condition. When this hazard is added to a plant that is stressed by water shortage, the problems can be magnified and the end result may be serious damage to the plant and possible death. The best initial protection against all pests and diseases is a strongly growing, healthy plant and all the points we have and will be making about encouraging good growth are very relevant.

Even with careful protection pests and diseases occur. Most gardeners adopting environmentally friendly responses to water usage will probably not wish to use chemical pest control. Although this may sometimes be the only solution to some problems, it should be the last resort. A garden that is based on good environmental principles should already have a good balance of natural pathogens and predators and, given time, the pest will be controlled naturally. So for example a small outbreak of aphids in summer will usually be controlled by ladybirds and lacewings.

If a pest or a disease develops on important plants or vegetable and fruit crops and you are unwilling to risk the interplay of natural agencies, there are other methods. Some pests and diseases can be controlled by importing additional predators and parasites, called biological controls. Many are tried and tested, and work very well. They are particularly effective in greenhouses and commercial sources for these predators and parasites are readily available. Alternatively you may wish to resort to a pesticide of some sort that is environmentally friendly. Products such as soft soap in liquid form will tackle a host of pests without harming the environment. Most pesticides nowadays will give an indication of their toxicity level and in fact most of those on sale for the private gardener are very safe both to the user and the environment.

Slugs and snails can be particular problems in the waterwise garden. During times of drought they will seem to disappear but will no doubt be living very successfully underneath the mulch that you have generously supplied. Damp weather will bring them out in force together with the damage they cause.

There are various techniques, gadgets and gizmos recommended for slugs, all of which have some varying level of success. However, the safest and soundest way of controlling these without toxic pesticides is by use of a biological agent. This contains microscopic nematodes which kill the slugs. There is no risk to children, pets or birds.

Weeds

Weeds are another fact of gardening life. They seem to appear everywhere and often to grow better than the plants we are trying to cultivate. They are nevertheless undesirable as they compete with our garden plants for nutrients and all important water. The more the weeds take up, the less there is

for our plants so keeping the waterwise garden free of weeds is an essential. Fortunately the whole procedure of mulching, which is likely to be in full use in such gardens, will also prevent the majority of weed growth. The main problem areas are likely to be those that are irrigated and do not have a mulch, areas such as the vegetable garden, pots and containers.

Some gardeners like to hoe off weeds and leave them on the surface to die, claiming they act as a 'weed mulch'. Such a practice is

BELOW Wherever they are in the garden, weeds will compete with other plants for all important water and should be removed.

generally untidy, is unlikely to be effective as a mulch and a proportion of the weeds are likely to root back in and re-grow. I'd avoid this one.

One definition of a weed is a 'plant in the wrong place' which may be so in terms of our gardens – they spring up just where we don't want them. One of the reasons why weeds are so successful is that they take advantage of the current conditions, so even in a drought there will be some weeds that will thrive and grow.

Feeding plants

All plants need nutrients to grow and develop and a healthy, well-fed plant is more likely to withstand adverse conditions than one that is weak and poorly nourished. The three main elements needed by plants are nitrogen, phosphorous and potassium (sometimes called potash) and generally referred to as NPK from their chemical symbols. These are required in large quantities for growth. Generally one thinks of nitrogen as the nutrient that promotes leaf growth, phosphorous for roots and potassium for flowers or fruit.

In addition, all plants require a range of other elements in differing levels. Magnesium (Mg), Calcium (Ca), and sulphur (S) are the next most important. Finally there are those

that are required in minute quantities and are usually called trace elements. These include Iron (Fe), manganese (Mn), copper (Cu), zinc (Zn), boron (Bo), molybdenum (Mb) and chlorine (Cl). There are many types of fertiliser that will contain varying amounts of all or some of these for different purposes. It is virtually never necessary to add sulphur as such, as it is normally present as part of other compounds such as ammonium sulphate.

Fertilisers

Nowadays there is a bewildering range of fertilisers available for use and products will be described in many different ways. Chemical or inorganic fertilisers are factory produced, generally cheap and are the type of fertilisers widely used in agriculture, for vegetable or fruit production or for fertilising lawns. Organic fertilisers originate from some sort of natural

BELOW Plants will usually tell us of nutrient deficiencies. The yellowing leaves on this rhododendron exhibit a lack of iron caused by a chalky soil.

product and include things such as bonemeal or dried blood. They will generally be more expensive and slower in reaction than chemical fertilisers as the material has to break down in the soil to release the nutrients.

You might occasionally come across straight fertilisers. These are generally rather outdated and rarely used nowadays. These will be simple chemicals providing one or two nutrients, for example Superphosphate, which is a phosphorous fertiliser. Much more likely will be fertilisers described as compound or balanced. These will have a blend of different nutrients within them supplying all of the plant's needs in one application. One of the commonest is 'Growmore', a cheap balanced chemical fertiliser widely used for vegetable production.

Slow-release fertilisers are the best type of fertilisers and will have all the nutrients required bound up in a small pill which breaks down slowly within the soil, feeding the plants over a predictable span of time. Such fertilisers are very useful in providing a whole season's nutrients in one application. Larger pellets or plugs of slow-release fertiliser are available for pot plants and even for young trees.

Liquid Feeds are soluble fertilisers that can be watered around the plant's root system. They may be sold as a concentrated liquid that is diluted or as a powder, that is dissolved before applying. In both cases they must be diluted with the correct amount of water before using. Liquid feeds have the advantage of being immediately accessible to the plant and so give a rapid response. They are particularly valuable for pot plants, summer planters or hanging baskets and fast-growing crops such as tomatoes. Foliar feeds are similar to liquid feeds but instead of applying to the roots, they

ABOVE When spread by hand, granular fertilizers should be applied carefully and evenly to ensure the correct rate of application.

are sprayed directly on to the leaves and rapidly assimilated. Great care needs to be taken not to scorch the foliage. They are most likely to be used to correct minor trace element deficiencies in things like fruit trees, where it would take a long time for root applications to work.

Many of these terms appear together because they describe different things about a fertiliser. So for example we could have a slow-release, inorganic fertiliser like many modern commercial products or an organic balanced fertiliser such as blood, fish and bone – a very smelly mixture of traditional constituents!

Fertilisers should never be applied to plants that are dry or stressed. Try to ensure that an adequate feeding programme takes place during the best growing season when there is adequate moisture in the soil. Whenever handling fertilisers it is wise to use rubber gloves. Fertilisers can cause dermatitis or make the skin very dry. When applying large quantities, for example with an allotment or lawn, it is wise to use a dust mask to avoid inhaling the finer particles.

Kitchen garden crops

Many fruit and vegetables have high water requirements, particularly if we want to maximize the yields. Initially the main aim should be to build up a soil in your kitchen garden that has a high water holding capacity. This is done by regular generous treatments with organic matter.

Vegetables

In the vegetable garden you are less likely to worry about the visual appearance, so using materials such as polythene or fabric mulches is an option. Many vegetables such as potatoes and sweet corn are tried and tested under this regime but we can experiment with others. Do be aware that mulches such as this provide

WHAT'S ON THE PACKET
By law all fertilisers have to be packaged with an analysis of the contents on the outside. It will usually have a three figure code, maybe 15-30-15, which refers to the relevant proportions of NPK. The packet will probably also have a detailed analysis of the percentage of each nutrient. This is useful to determine whether trace elements are present or not.

The packet should also have a rate of application or for dilution in the case of liquid fertilisers. You should always read the instructions and never exceed the rates recommended. Applying a half-rate application then repeating at a later stage can be useful if there is any concern about causing scorch.

ideal hiding places for slugs so make provision to control these. It can be so disappointing to peel back a polythene mulch and find a bumper crop of potatoes all damaged by slugs.

Horticultural fleece is another woven material that is translucent and allows light to penetrate. It is generally used to cover young crops such as tender salads or sweetcorn and give minimal protection from cold. It is also beneficial to crops such as carrots, which need protection from pests such as carrot root fly. It has a secondary value in reducing water loss when the crop is young and little of the soil is covered by foliage. At this stage water loss direct from the soil by evaporation can be high.

With some vegetables, water can be directed at various stages of production. For example winter vegetables such as Brussels sprouts, cabbages and leeks will be planted in mid summer when the soil may be dry. Initially the plants can just be 'puddled' in by just watering the area immediately around each plant.

Other crops have specific water requirements such as peas, which need to be kept moist between flowering and harvest. Runner beans will not set their pods if they are dry at the roots during the flowering stage. Fruits such as strawberries and tomatoes have a particular need for water as the fruit is swelling and ripening. However too much water may make these fruits large but also bland and watery. Potatoes respond best when the flowers are just showing, which coincides with swelling of the tubers.

Irrigation in the vegetable garden should also be targeted very carefully with the equipment we use. Seephose or layflat tubing can be laid along rows and so target specific crops at sensitive times. Overhead sprinklers just do

not do this and you will end up watering the whole plot rather than just the crops that need it. Make sure that water does not run off into paths where it will be lost or possibly stimulate the growth of weeds. You can even use traditional furrow irrigation by planting your vegetables in a shallow depression and flooding water into this alone. This doesn't require any fancy equipment at all – just a spade.

Where there are paths in the vegetable garden, cover these to prevent water loss. Polythene will not be suitable as it will be slippery to work on but something such as bark or woodchips will prevent water loss from this non-productive area. Grass, although traditional will be taking water from the soil so better avoided. As with any other area of the garden, avoid excess weed growth in the vegetable plot as all weeds will compete with your crops for water.

ABOVE Potatoes growing through this polythene mulch will have no competition from weeds and there is no light to discolour the tubers.

Some crops are more tolerant of limited water and these include root crops such as carrots, beetroot, parsnips and turnips, all of which have deep tap roots. Onions are also tolerant. Plant breeders are working on developing crops that will tolerate low water requirements but this may mean changes to vegetables that are not as yet familiar in European gardens and kitchens.

If you have an area of the vegetable garden that is not being used in summer, sow a green manure crop. These are available from seed merchants and are mixes of fast growing plants, some of which will fix nitrogen in the soil. When you are next ready to use that piece of land the green manure is dug in. All the nutrients and moisture that the green manure has absorbed are then returned to the soil for re-use by your next crop. As the green manure breaks down it will also provide a source of organic matter to further improve the water-holding capacity of your soil.

Fruit

Fruits are in most cases more than 90 per cent water so their demands for water will be high. For example, small plants such as strawberries, which are replaced every two or three years, will have only a limited, shallow rootsystem and so will not produce good crops without adequate readily, available water.

However, at the other extreme, established apple or pear trees will have an exten-

sive, deep reaching root system able to tap into deep soil reserves of water and still provide a reasonable crop even in dry summers. As private gardeners we will be less interested in the overall yield but may find that smaller apples or pears will have a better flavour. The same could be said of other tree fruits such as plums or cherries.

Bush fruits such as blackcurrants, redcurrants and gooseberries will come somewhere in between the tree fruits and strawberry examples. They will have an established rootsystem but this will tend to be shallower than that of a tree so they will be more prone to water stress. Raspberries in particular respond badly to a shortage of water from flowering through to ripening. All types of fruit respond well to a good thick heavy mulch applied before the soil starts to dry in the spring.

BELOW The straw around these strawberries will keep the ripening fruit off the soil and also help to retain moisture in the soil.

Waterwise lawns

A smooth, verdant, bowling green style lawn is to many the epitome of a well manicured garden and successful gardener. Such a landscape feature, as attractive as it may be, will require vast quantities of water to keep it in tip-top condition. Lawn grasses are amongst the thirstiest plants in the garden. If you are serious about a waterwise garden, you will need to rethink the role that grass plays in your landscape. Although lawns are a very real part of many gardens providing a neutral foil and a recreational area, there are other alternatives.

Think carefully where you really need grass, maybe a play area for children or somewhere to sit on a hot day. In other parts of the garden it may be possible to replace it with gravel or with another living green foil. Plants such as thyme and prostrate juniper will provide a carpet effect and remain green in conditions of drought when grass would not. Thyme will even take a certain amount of foot traffic but don't expect it to stand up to a football match.

Many of us will still want some 'real' grass. It may be that a reduced size lawn will be adequate whilst we develop some of the space in different ways. Think about tailoring your lawn to the sprinkler you might use to keep it green. For example a single rotary sprinkler would efficiently irrigate a circular lawn with no waste, and an oscillating sprinkler would suit a rectangular area.

In evry case, consider how you maintain your lawn. Instead of collecting the clippings when mowing, allow these to fly and return to the surface. Such material will act as a mulch and help retain moisture. Allow clover to develop or even overseed to add this to a sward. Clover stays green in a drought, when

most lawn grasses go yellow and brown. Clover also has the amazing ability to fix nitrogen, an essential plant nutrient, from the air, which it releases into the soil and so will feed itself and nearby grasses. It's a win-win plant. There is the issue of flowering clover attracting bees, so this may not be advisable in gardens with children or if you like to go barefoot.

Gardeners in wetter climates have not previously had to worry about the types of grass we used for lawns as drought has not been an issue, but this is no longer the case. One of the lawn grass breeders has now developed a drought resistant lawn grass, called Rhizomatous Tall Fescue, specifically

ARTIFICIAL GRASS

And what about artificial grass? This is the synthetic carpet style material that is used for all-weather sports pitches. I can almost hear the purists groaning. Well, let's consider this for what it is. As an alternative to an emerald green lawn it is certainly a very false looking alternative. Grass is, however, just an outdoor carpet. At a distance artificial grass will give a semblance of green. Now this may not be acceptable as part of a high quality landscape but I would argue that it could have a place particularly in the family garden where a safe, hard wearing play surface is required.

We could also add that it does not require water, so is perfectly acceptable in our waterwise garden. What is more, if this product is bough second-hand there is an element of environmental-friendliness. The specialists that install these pitches will have to pay high costs to have the old carpets disposed of to landfill and may well be quite happy to sell quantities for a low price.

LAWN RESCUE

A traditional lawn that has suffered badly in a summer drought will probably be yellow or brown by autumn. It may also have bare patches and some weeds that have grown more vigorously than we would wish. The first rains of the autumn will result in some natural recovery and it is amazing how many grasses will revive from what appears to be a dead state. However the sward will be thin and weak. This is the opportunity to give it some tender loving care to encourage it back to health again. In hot countries such autumn renovation is a normal and essential annual procedure.

First rake out all the dead grass using a wire rake or a mechanised scarifier. Follow this with spiking to allow air and water into the soil. This can be done with a fork or there are specialised machines available to do this. Ideally you will then topdress with a very thin layer of sieved soil which is worked in amongst the grasses with a rake or brush. If there are really bare patches these can be oversown with grass seed at this stage. Finally a fertiliser can be used. A low-nitrogen fertiliser should be selected that will not encourage excess winter growth. Such a treatment will usually bring most lawns back into a pristine condition for the winter and better able to withstand at least some summer stress the next year.

for our altered conditions. This performs well in drought, doesn't mind being water-logged or frozen in winter, is shade tolerant and incredibly hard wearing. Its still very new but is likely to have a great future. Despite its name, it makes a close knit sward, which spreads and colonizes well. Its deep rhizomatous root system is the key to its drought tolerance.

Flowering meadows

In recent years there has been a move away from close mown grass towards meadowlands with all the bonuses of wildflowers and other wildlife, such as birds and butterflies, that it will attract. Such areas are totally different in appearance and need altered maintenance but are very environmentally sound and will not require any additional water.

If you are starting a meadow from scratch, this can be done by seeding with a suitable mix of wildflowers and native grasses. Allowing an existing lawn to just grow into a meadowland may be disappointing as it may not have sufficient diversity to provide interest. This will be particularly so if weedkillers have been used to remove broad-leaved weeds, which ironically we now want to encourage for a meadow. In this situation, small plug plants of wildflowers can be purchased and added to the existing sward to provide greater interest. Before planting scrape away the surface grasses to form a small clear circle before planting at least 20 cm (8 in) in diameter. This will allow the new plant the chance to establish without undue competition.

LEFT Small circular lawns such as these in this desert garden can be irrigated efficiently by single sprinklers.
BELOW This wildflower meadow illustrates the wealth of colour and interest possible when we stop close mowing of lawns.

57

Meadows are not mown regularly, although you may decide to mow access paths through them to give you somewhere to walk or you may decide to continue to mow a small area near your house for recreational purposes. The main cut for a meadow should take place in midsummer. This allows most of the plant and other lifecycles to run to completion. It is very important to remove the mowings from a meadow and these can be composted. If you do not remove them, the thick cut grass will smother the regenerating wildflowers and in time you will have nothing except coarse grasses. Mowing a meadow in this way can be quite a heavy job but it is only once per year, compared to the many times that you would mow a traditional lawn.

Annuals for the dry garden

Annuals are excellent plants for the waterwise garden. The initial cost is a packet of seeds and a little time. Their life cycles are short and they will maximise available water with rapid growth. If subsequent drought in later summer causes early death, there is really no loss as they are one season plants anyway.

Most hardy annuals will germinate at quite low temperatures so they should be sown in early spring when the soil is still moist, giving them have many weeks to grow and establish before conditions become dry. They are usually sown directly in a prepared seedbed outside. Some of the really tough ones can be sown in the autumn and will survive winter as small but sturdy seedlings. If you prefer, annuals can be sown in pots or small modules in a cool greenhouse and then planted out, but this should take place as soon as possible to catch this period of maximum establishment.

Although some bedding plants aren't genuinely annuals, they are treated as such and thrown away at the end of the season. Most are tender and so are raised under glass and planted out in late spring after the danger of frost. Unless the weather is naturally wet, they will all require some water for establishment . The waterwise gardener should choose species that will require minimal water after the initial settling in period.

RIGHT Garden centres stock many drought tolerant plants such as these lovely old olive trees with their gnarled trunks.

DROUGHT-TOLERANT
HARDY ANNUALS
- *Amaranthus cruentus* 'Love Lies Bleeding'
- *Calendula officinalis* 'Geisha Girl'
- *Dimorphotheca aurantiaca* 'Star of the Veldt'
- *Eschscholzia californica* (Californian poppies in many cultivars)
- *Helianthus annuus* (sunflower in many cultivars)
- *Molucella laevis* (Bells of Ireland)
- *Nigella damascena* (Love in a mist)
- *Papaver nudicaule* 'Meadow Pastels' (Iceland Poppies)
- *Phacelia viscida*

Container gardening

For many of us, large pots, hanging baskets and window boxes form key parts of our garden layouts. They may contain favourite plants that come out from our conservatories for the summer or they may be special planters in key locations designed to give impact. Containers not only dry out quicker than the soil itself but will also be more likely to heat up in the summer sunshine and chill in winter frost. For this reason use as large a container as you can to give more even growing conditions. Although these will undoubtedly need certain levels of watering as the soil they contain will be limited, there are various things we can do to make them more water efficient.

Initially fill containers with a good potting compost. Although there are many multi-purpose composts available today, the waterwise gardener is better to choose a loam based compost which will be slower to dry out. Mix water-retaining granules in with the compost when you are filling the containers and leave a good space at the top so that watering can be accomplished without spilling and wasting water.

Many of the plants we might traditionally choose for containers are very thirsty plants and it may be that you will decide that this is one area where you cannot compromise. However there are a number of colourful plants that will grow and thrive in containers with minimal watering and still give us a striking display.

Containers should, if possible, be grouped in a logical sequence making it possible to easily water them with minimal effort. Remember that with a hosepipe ban you are likely to have to do this with a

DROUGHT TOLERANT CONTAINER PLANTS

- Arctotis
- *Astelia nervosa*
- *Centaurea gymnocarpa*
- *Cordyline australis*
- Echevaria
- *Eucalyptus gunnii*
- Euphorbia
- French Marigold
- Gazania
- Grasses
- Ivy leaved geraniums
- Osteospermum
- *Phormium tenax*
- Petunia
- Yucca

watering can. If you are going to install a micro-bore drip system It also makes sense to have containers near each other or in a sequence around the house. Stand pots in saucers wherever possible so that drainage

SECTION TWO

water is not lost but remains as a reservoir for later use.

Hanging baskets are very sensitive to water in the past may have been watered these on a daily basis. To many of us these balls of summer colour are a key feature of our gardens and we may wish to continue to try and grow them. If this is so, there are various things that can be done to reduce the water requirements. Ideally choose a plastic basket with a built-in water reservoir. They may not be so attractive but with good planting the container can be hidden.

Alternatively, line your basket with polythene rather than traditional moss, and put holes around the side for drainage but not right in the bottom. This will leave a small part of the lining which will hold water for later use. Don't forget to add water retaining granules to the compost.

Select your plants carefully and use those such as ivy leaved pelargoniums, helichryssum, gazanias, marigold and portu-

BELOW French Marigolds, *Helichryssum petiolare*, and the less known *Euryops chrysanthemoides* are excellent summer bedding plants that perform well without extra water.

DROGHT TOLERANT BEDDING PLANTS

**DROUGHT TOLERANT
BEDDING PLANTS**

- *Alyssum maritimum* 'Carpet of Snow' (sweet alyssum)
- *Arctotis hybrida* (several named cultivars – African Daisy)
- *Briza maxima* (Quaking grass)
- *Cleome spinosa* 'Colour Fountain' (spider flower)
- *Cosmos bipinnatus* 'Sonata Mixed'
- *Gazania* 'Kiss Series' (treasure flower)
- *Helichryssum petiolare*
- *Lavatera trimestris* 'Silver Cup' (annual mallow)
- *Limonium sinuatum* (statice)
- *Mesembryanthemum criniflorum* (Livingstone daisy)
- *Osteospermum hybrida* (Star of the Veldt)
- Petunia (many cultivars)
- *Portulaca grandiflora* (sun plant)
- *Rudbeckia hirta* 'Marmalade' (coneflower)
- *Salvia splendens* 'Blaze of Fire'
- *Salvia farinacea* 'Victoria'
- *Senecio cineraria* 'Silver Dust' (Dusty Miller)
- *Tagetes erecta* (African marigold – many cultivars)
- *Tagetes patula* (French Marigold – many cultivars)
- *Verbena bonariensis*
- *Zinnia elegans* 'Parasol Mixed'

Herbs and aromatic plants

Many herbs and aromatic foliage plants naturally originate from Mediterranean areas such as the chaparral where water is restricted so will grow and thrive in our waterwise garden. Subjects such as thyme, sage and lavender will thrive in dry parched gritty soils in full sun. Under such conditions their aromatic oils and their flavour will also be particularly pronounced. All of the following will thrive in a waterwise garden:

- *Thymus vulgaris* (thyme – many cultivars available)
- *Rosmarinus officinalis* (rosemary)
- *Salvia officinalis* (sage)
- *Laurus nobilis* (sweet bay)
- *Melissa officinalis* (lemon balm)
- *Origanum marjorana* (sweet marjoram)
- *Artemesia dracunculus* (French tarragon)
- *Petroselinum neopolitanum* (Italian parsley)
- *Satureja hortensis* (summer savoury)

Position them near the house where they can be easily accessed for use in the kitchen. Small enclosed garden areas will also concentrate the perfumes which will be held in the air on sunny days.

As well as those grown for culinary use, there are several aromatic plants worth growing, just for their garden value. *Pevovskia* 'Blue spire', Lavenders, *Ruta gravaeolens*, *Lippia citriodora*, *Artemesia* 'Powis Castle' and of course all the *Eucalyptus* are all drought tolerant and have fragrant foliage.

laca, which are less water demanding. Avoid impatiens, begonia and fuchsia. Position hanging baskets so that drips will land on plants or other containers that will benefit from the excess water, rather than it just going to waste. All these little points may seem marginal but added together they make a great deal of difference in the water-wise garden.

RIGHT Smokey grasses contrast well with brightly coloured herbaceous plants in this closely planted little garden.

Intelligent irrigation

Virtually all keen gardeners, however conscientious about water usage, will need to water some plants and parts of their gardens at times. The following pages explain how to apply water most efficiently, when to water and the best tools for intelligent irrigation. This may be either mains water (if there is no hosepipe ban), stored rainwater or recycled grey water, as discussed in Section One. However you choose to water your garden, a responsible approach is vital to be truely waterwise.

Hand watering

We must have all seen gardeners holding a hose, in the full sun of a blazing hot day, and lightly spraying over the surface of everything in sight. Such irrigation does no good at all. Very little of the water will be reaching the roots; in fact some will evaporate before it even reaches the soil. Such gardeners are often seen repeating this futile ritual on a daily basis. Very few areas of the garden need daily watering.

At the other extreme you will sometimes see sprinklers running for hours at a time, spraying water high into the air before it lands on the ground. Such an exercise may achieve the end result of soaking the soil but it is very wasteful of water as it is totally indiscriminate and doesn't target important areas. An average garden sprinkler can use as much as 300 litres (65 gallons) of water in just 30 minutes. Also overhead sprinklers will always mean a loss of water by evaporation.

Watering individual plants by means of a watering can or open hosepipe is a valid technique. Where we have things like newly planted trees so that water can be directed where it is most needed. Simple aids can be used to make this technique more effective.

Purpose-made watering units are available for trees. These consist of a length of perforated pipe that is installed when the tree is planted. It is wrapped around the tree's root-system before the topsoil is finally replaced. The end of the pipe protrudes above ground level and water can be directed straight into this and down to the area where the young roots are developing. A similar technique is to sink a plastic flower pot into the ground next to a plant that is likely to need watering. Filling this transports the water under the surface to the rooting zone of the plant.

Traditionally, vulnerable trees were often planted with a saucer-like depression at the surface. Although this does help to direct the applied water, it is still on the surface and has to percolate to the rooting zone so is less effective than the techniques described above.

RIGHT When planting a tree either a purpose made watering device or even a simple length of drainpipe will help future watering needs.

This method may be valuable, however, for planting on a bank where the water might readily run away before percolating.

Irrigation systems

These can be divided into drip or spray systems and drip systems may be above or below ground. Many of the modern systems have very efficient water usage but may not be permitted when there is a hosepipe ban as technically they are regarded as being part of a hosepipe system. Micro-bore drip systems will use far less water than a watering can but still may not be permitted during a ban.

Leaky pipe systems consist of a length of plastic or rubber piping that either has numerous small holes throughout its length or may be made of a material that is naturally porous. The piping is usually laid on the soil surface. When connected to a water supply the water oozes out slowly throughout its length, supplying water directly to the soil surface. Because of the minimal exposure to the air, there is little chance of loss by evaporation. Such systems are ideal for plants such as vegetables, cut flowers or nursery stock that are in rows. They can be used for planted borders where the pipes will be zig-zagged through the planting and can be covered by an ornamental mulch. 'T' junctions and other connectors are available for more complex areas.

A cheaper and less effective version of this is known as lay-flat tubing. It consists of thin polythene tubing that is perforated at regular intervals. It comes as a flat material that is rolled-up. When unrolled and connected to a water supply, the tubing inflates and then produces a series of very fine jets. As there is some exposure to the air before the water hits

the ground there is likely to be some loss by means of evaporation, but it is still a fairly efficient system at a low cost.

Microbore irrigation

These systems are based on small diameter pipes that supply water to exactly the area required. They are particularly useful for hanging baskets and groups of planters or containers with crops such as tomatoes or cucumbers. They are equally effective when used in out in the open or in greenhouses.

KNOW YOUR HOSE

Whatever type of irrigation is used a length of hosepipe is usually needed for connection. Cheap garden hose is not a good investment. It will quickly kink and cause repeated annoyance, when the water flow is blocked and it snags around your legs. Buy a good reinforced hose and it will probably have anything up to a twenty-year guarantee. A good hose will be made up of several layers – a smooth inner layer, a reinforced woven layer then the outer layer.

Buy a reel of some sort to store it on. These can be simple racks on the wall on which you coil the hose or a more sophisticated version which will enable you to wind up the hose with a handle or even portable versions that can be moved around. Many of the irrigation systems and sprinklers have quick release couplings that enable you to change from one piece of irrigation equipment to another so its worth selecting your brand and sticking to it.

Remember also that by law all outdoor taps for use with garden hoses must have a non-return valve fitted to avoid any contaminated water flowing back into the drinking water system.

ABOVE A microbore dropper such as this is unobtrusive and yet will carefully supply adequate water with no waste to this potted plant.

Irrigation suppliers offer a range of different kits containing all the components to make up a suitable system for various numbers of pots or baskets.

These systems consist of a supply pipe that runs the full length of the area you want to irrigate. Small diameter 'microtubes' are then connected and run to each of the containers we wish to water. This is usually terminated by a 'dripper' although it can be a small sprinkler head. These may have a variable output and can be adjusted or may be fixed. You can also vary the number of drippers to a container depending on its size. So with a group of mixed sized planters you might have some larger ones with two or three drippers and some small ones with a single one in each.

You can find out how much water the drippers supply by running the system with some empty containers, such as jam jars, underneath the drippers and then timing it accordingly. One disadvantage of microbore systems is that they can become easily blocked and you should not use them with grey water or any supplies that might not be totally pure, without prior filtering.

Irrigation controls

A microbore system is dependant on being used for a carefully measured time and indeed any waterwise irrigation system needs to be timed to apply the optimum amount of water without waste. There are now a number of

WATER PRESSURE

Some irrigation systems may require you to know the pressure of your water supply. This is not always easy for the amateur to ascertain. You may have to ask your water supply company or your plumber. More commonly you may need to know the flow. This is easily ascertained by turning a tap or hose on to full and measuring how long it takes to fill a standard 9 litre (2 gallon) bucket. Use the following formula to calculate the litres per hour:

$$\text{Litres per hour} = \frac{9 \times 3600}{\text{Time in seconds}}$$

Work this out before you go to a store to buy an irrigation system or you may have a fruitless journey.

timers and programmers that can be obtained to control irrigation systems such as microbore and leaky hose set-ups. Simple clockwork timers will simply turn off the water after a certain period of time. Use them to measure the amount of water applied but avoid using them to schedule watering regularly. This inevitably results in watering too often. Use the system only when it is needed. Having the option to schedule watering can however be useful for when you are on holiday.

Others timers are based on a small battery powered programmer and will allow for one or more periods of watering each day at a determined time and for a set duration. Such programmers take the guess-work out of irrigation and allow the use of water at night.

LEFT Group planters together for maximum effect and to make watering easier whether by hand or by an automated system.

Calculating irrigation quantities

There are no easy answers to the very basic question "How often do I water this?". Within the plant world there are so many different plants with different water requirements that will vary according to the conditions of the gardens, homes and greenhouses that host them. Getting watering right is both a tricky and crucial skill which is really only fully acquired with experience. A few pointers are given below.

With any irrigation system, or indeed with manual watering, it is always best to water until the soil is moist right through the rooting zone. With container-grown plants this is easy to judge as excess water will run out of the bottom of the pot when the soil is fully wet. With plants growing in the ground this is more difficult to assess so it is worth digging a small 'inspection pit' after irrigating to see how far the water has percolated.

You should aim to supply sufficient water to completely moisten the rooting zone, which will vary depending on the type of plants you are growing. For example a crop of lettuce will have roots that only penetrate a few inches into the ground, but fruit trees will have a much deeper rootzone. One common mistake is to apply too little water, too frequently. The result of this will be excess shallow rooting. Such surface roots will suffer quickly if there is any interruption in watering. Encouraging a deep root system means that plants can tap into water reserves that do not fluctuate so frequently. In general it is better to provide one heavy watering a week than light watering every night.

Every type of irrigation equipment is best used when conditions are cool and the air still to avoid unnecessary evaporation. Never irrigate during windy conditions.

SECTION THREE
The Aesthetics

Planning the waterwise garden

Garden design must always be based on aesthetics. Aiming to create a garden that is pleasing to look at and satisfying to be in is what gardening is all about. Many of our ideas on garden design will be based on favourite public gardens, glimpses of private gardens and those fabulous theatrical gardens created for flower shows. Our ideas may be stereotyped so in this section we will look beyond that as we plan the waterwise garden.

Designing for drought

Only in recent years have gardeners in traditionally wetter climates to think about how gardens will fare in dry weather or the extremes of a drought or heatwave. Such conditions in the past have been so rare in these areas that when they occurred gardeners could turn the hose on and wait for the weather to cool down. Now that water for gardening purposes is so much more restricted we must consider how the layout of our gardens can be arranged to make the maximum use of what little water we have.

IDEAS FROM OVERSEAS
Many of the pictures and some of the ideas published in this book will refer to gardens in other countries and climates. In temperate areas we are only recently coming to terms with the idea of a hot dry climate becoming more common but in many countries this has been the norm for a long time. We can therefore learn a great deal from how gardeners deal with heat and drought in other countries.

We have two choices. We can continue designing traditional gardens that may be less than successful in a dry summer with the risk of a parched, burnt-out look, or we can really get to grips with the issues of water restrictions and plan a garden that is likely to survive and thrive in the increasingly frequent hot summers. It's not necessarily better but it will be different and likely to be more successful.

Many other principles will come into the design equation – matters such as cost, time available to maintain the garden, family needs, personal plant preferences and so on. These will all govern what we put in our gardens and how we arrange them.

Zoning a new garden

Gardeners who have gardened in drier climates are used to the concept of zoning a garden, but for many of us this will be a new idea. Zoning quite simply means grouping plants and features in your garden that need similar

RIGHT This desert garden at The Old Vicarage, East Ruston, England, shows the wonderful contrast between the stark stone surfaces and lush green planting.

quantities of water. These areas are called water zones, or sometimes hydrozones. Zoning a garden according to its water needs is relatively straightforward when laying out a garden from scratch, but less easy where we have an existing garden to adapt. We will approach the subject as if working on a blank canvas and then consider later how we might adapt an existing garden.

Some of the fashionable garden styles automatically fall into certain zones so it's not as difficult as it may seem. For example, if you have created a gravel garden already then you have a low water zone, and if you are planning a prairie border this usually falls neatly into the medium water zone. The current exotic style of gardening with lush plantings of bananas, cannas and other foliage is likely to fall into the high water zone. With a little careful planning a successfully zoned garden is achievable.

Low water zone

A low water zone would be an area where plants survive mostly on natural rainfall and are unlikely to suffer with drought and high temperatures. These would include succulent plants, silver foliage and spiky plants such as yucca. They will tolerate full sun and a dry gravelly soil yet still thrive. As well as these desert-style plants there are some quite familiar garden trees, shrubs and herbaceous plants that will tolerate very dry conditions without showing undue stress.

The soil should be well prepared and well drained as there are likely to be plants that will not tolerate any degree of waterlogging. Even though these plants will tolerate dry conditions it is still worth while mulching

BELOW Positioning groups of plants with higher water requirements close to a water source makes for efficient watering in this zoned garden.

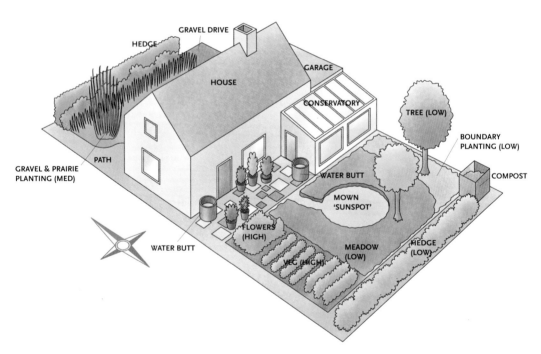

the soil surface with gravel or some similar inorganic material.

Low water zones can be as extensive as you wish in a garden, as they are likely to be low maintenance. This will mean not only low watering but less weeding. Slower growth is also likely to mean fewer activities such as trimming and pruning. Although there is no reason why you cannot position low water zones anywhere, it makes some sense to have them further away from your house, retaining areas closer to your home for zones needing some water.

Such low maintenance refers only to established plants and it is worth noting that all new plantings will require enough water to develop good root systems over at least the first season, before they can become independent.

Medium water zone

Plants for a medium water zone would consist of ornamental grasses, prairie plants, many shrubs and some trees. They will thrive in sunny conditions, prefer a slightly richer, moisture holding soil and will require some occasional watering in prolonged dry weather. A high proportion of hardy garden plants in temperate areas will fall into this category.

Soils need to be well prepared for these plantings with generous dressings of organic matter mixed through a deep, well cultivated rootzone. The soil is most likely to be surfaced with an organic material. Bark, for example, would work very well.

Many trees, shrubs and roses fall into the medium water zone with a proportion of herbaceous plants. Traditionally these plantings only need watering when they are young and establishing or during severe drought

conditions. Otherwise they are normally quite content and will survive through short periods of water shortage as well as the extremes of winter wet and cold. They are generally very tolerant, easy plants.

High water zone

A high water zone will include soft, lush plants such as vegetables, fruits, many herbaceous perennials and lawns that will need constant and regular watering to maintain an active, healthy state of growth. Loams and soils with a higher clay content will generally be more suitable for such plants as they will tend to hold moisture naturally. There will of course be exceptions. For example, carrots grow best on light sandy soils and will tolerate drought but prefer adequate quantities of water to grow well. It can be confusing.

High water zone plantings are likely to need a rich, well prepared soil that is high in organic matter and will promote fast lush growth. Most of the plants placed here will grow quickly, and some such as vegetables or bedding plants will complete their life cycle in a single season so they need conditions which allow unchecked growth.

High water zone plants are in many ways luxury plants for the waterwise gardener. Gardens will generally be planned around low and medium water zones, but there may be some desirable plants that do not fit into these categories. Personally I could not do without a couple of lush potted banana plants and a few cannas to add a hint of the tropics to my garden. Position your High Water Zone near to the house where there is a water source and use responsible irrigation as far as possible.

Maximising water use

Grouping similar types of plants together is the easiest way to manage a garden in dry weather and make the maximum use of small quantities of water. The practicalities of zoning will start with soil preparation and the soil in each zone can be prepared for the plants they are to receive. Good soil-enriching organic matter is always in short supply and you can make the best use of this by concentrating this on high and medium water zone areas.

When additional water needs to be used by means of irrigation this is going to be much easier if it can be directed to one area rather than dragging heavy hoses all round the garden to water odd plants here and there. Mixing together low and high water zone plants makes little sense and hard work for any gardener.

Zoning an existing garden

Zoning an existing mature garden is more difficult and only partial results may be possible. It might be helpful to make a sketch of the garden and colour-in the water requirements of the existing plants and features. You will then see if there are any patterns. If there are concentrations of drought tolerant plants in certain areas you may be able to strengthen this by moving around other plants and removing any that have high water requirements. This will obviously be impossible with large shrubs or mature trees, but some rationalization is achievable even though it may not be as logical as with a newly designed garden.

LEFT The author's small town garden with a low water shrubby background and pots of luxury exotics near the house.

Microclimates

All gardens will have spots in which the conditions are slightly different to those in the surrounding areas – we call these microclimates. Some will be unfavourable, such as cold windy corners or very shady areas. However when we get to know these in our garden, we should treat them as part of our zoning system.

For example there may be an area close to your house where the rain just never

BELOW The Oregan Grape is a tough evergreen groundcover plant with yellow flowers that will tolerate the most daunting of dry shady situations.

PLANTS FOR DRY SHADE
- *Cortaderia selloana* (pampas grass)
- *Euonymus fortunei* (various coloured leaved cultivars)
- *Cotoneaster* (many species and cultivars)
- *Hedera* (ivy in all its many forms)
- *Iris foetidissima* (stinking iris)
- *Mahonia aquifolium* (Oregon grape)
- *Prunus laurocerasus* 'Cherry Brandy'
- *Rubus calycinoides* and *R. tricolour*
- *Salvia officinalis* (sage and the coloured leaved forms)
- *Santolina chamaecyparissus* (cotton lavender)

seems to penetrate and is permanently dry – a 'rain shadow'. Such an area needs to be part of our low water zone. Don't fight the conditions but go with them, choosing plants that will grow and thrive in such a sun baked spot. Plant some succulents, or gamble on cacti. Some gardens might have a low spot that remains damp when other parts of the garden have dried out. Use this spot for plants needing medium or high water levels and this will reduce the need for irrigation, making your job easier.

Shade is often regarded as a problem in a garden but can offer different opportunities. Most shady sites will not be as hot or as dry as their sunny counterparts. There are many different plants that will grow and thrive in shady areas and are not just tolerant of but prefer reduced light levels.

The most difficult shady areas are those under the shade of large trees. This is a problem spot with compound restrictions of shade and dry, impoverished soils that are compacted with heavy root runs. Even in such inhospitable locations, however, there are some real pioneers that will bravely provide some vegetation. I have seen some very attractive gardens where the area under a large tree is carpeted with plain green ivy, echoing the shape of the tree's canopy, and acting as a sort of green shadow. A pattern of such overlapping shapes can be striking in a simple way.

Equally it may be more appropriate to use some areas of deep shade for alternative garden treatments. This might take the form of some sort of attractive mulch like cobbles, pine cones or slate. This treatment is environmentally sound and retains what moisture there is for the use of the tree.

Gardening without plants

A typical dictionary definition of a garden is a planned space, usually outdoors, set aside for the display, cultivation, and enjoyment of plants. This is familiar to most of us who view our gardens as a green verdant place where we grow things, but this is only part of the story. Most gardens consist of components other than plants. Different cultures view gardens in various ways. At the opposite end of the spectrum to the typical plant-abundant gardens are minimalist and symbolic landscapes, such as Zen gardens, with few, if any, plants. Relating this to a waterwise garden it is important to include as many non-plant features as possible, giving added interest to our garden without the restraints of water availability.

BELOW A few well chosen plants can be quite striking in an otherwise architectural landscape.

Floors and walls

Within a garden there are many surfaces, both flat and vertical. When designing, it is important to ensure that paths and ground surfaces are more than just utilitarian places to walk but features in themselves. There are many different types of attractive paving available which can be laid in a myriad of combinations and patterns. Gone are the days when all that was available were concrete slabs. As well as the many different types of artificial stone, there is cut natural stone and a whole host of block paviers. Additonally you might want to consider timber decking.

Do remember that uninterrupted paving can be very hot and dry. Break up areas of paving with blocks of planting. Include trees and pergolas to provide shade and greenery.

We have spoken elsewhere about all the many types of gravel (page 4) but it is appropriate to mention it again here as a consideration. There is also the possibility of raked sand and the patterns that could be created. This may seem a bit far-fetched to our Western eyes but many gardeners will methodically mow their lawns to create a pattern of stripes, so why not raked sand?

Vertical surfaces are just as important. The boundaries of our gardens need not be plain wooden fences. Different types of wooden panels are available and various coloured stains can be used to give different effects. The boundary of choice would for many people be a mellow red brick wall, but while this does give a sort of traditional classiness to a garden it may not always be appropriate. Brick is of course expensive. Concrete blocks are cheaper and there's the option of finishing them with a stone paint to give a colour wash. This colour can of course be changed just as we redecorate our homes.

As well as the boundaries there many other vertical structures we can include in our gardens for interest. All manner of trellises, pergolas, archways, screens, railings and divisions are possible to give interest or divide the garden into smaller spaces. Gateways and arches will lead the eye from one area to another and mirrors will give an illusion of extra space. A book of garden designs or constructions will you some ideas.

Features

Having looked at creating gardens without plants, there are many things that can be added without the need for water. Garden furniture is becoming increasingly popular. At one time it was said that Italians designed gardens to sit in, as it was too hot to work, but the English designed gardens to work in, as it was too cold to sit. In recent summers, the sales of garden furniture in traditionally cooler regions has soared. Most of us want somewhere to sit outside and a table and chairs to make outdoor dining possible. Again many designs are available in timber or metal, both classical and modern. As well as being useful and, hopefully, comfortable garden furniture can be an attractive feature in its own right, even when not in use.

Garden ornaments, sculptures and statues may seem like a step away from gardening for many of us, but such features have been used in gardens throughout the ages. Anything is possible, from the simplest of items, such as fascinating pieces of driftwood and antique chimney posts, through to real statues or the or garden gnomes. Its your garden – why not have what you want! Garden centres will offer a range of such items or you can scour reclamation stores for architectural salvage.

Colour in the garden

So far we've not said much about colour. Everything has colour, although when we usually speak of colour in the garden we are usually thinking of the brighter, more dominant colours rather than the muted natural colours of greens, browns and greys. The colour from flowering plants is fleeting – it comes for a season and goes. Foliage plants are more likely to give longer lasting colour, particularly those that are evergreen. For this reason we need to be very careful how we site evergreens with very bright golden foliage. Plants such as the golden-leaved Elaeagnus look fabulous when first planted but may become overwhelming when the develop into a big brash bush five years later.

What we are really covering in this section is garden components other than plants, but the same principles apply here. Choose colours carefully and use sparingly. For a while there was a fashion for blue wood stain – fences, trellises, decking and walls all turned blue. Why just blue, I have no idea. There is a fabulous palette of colours available for using on garden features. I have a nasty concrete block wall at the bottom of my garden in the UK and I have painted this a soft terracotta red to remind me of the colours so regularly used in California. Using paints or wood stains on inanimate objects enables us to include colours in our landscapes which we might not be able to provide from plants, and certainly not in the same quantities of intensities. Use bright colours sparingly but boldly. This may seem a contradiction, but imagine a large container, painted a rich dark purple planted with a

silvery leaved Astelia. Some would say the container detracts from the plant, but does that matter if the overall effect gives pleasure? I don't think so.

Light

Light and colour interact constantly and colours will seem different in varying light conditions. Plants need different levels of light to grow and will often look best displayed under certain light levels. For example, dark colours and deep rich purple foliage look drab and boring in the shade but can be spectacular in bright sunshine. Sunlight that has filtered through foliage or a screen can give fascinating patterns and attractive shadows. Its only often only when the sun is shining brightly that we realise how striking shadow patterns can be. Light is also affected by air movement. A slight breeze will move leaves and alter the light patterns on them. Many waterwise plants have silvery undersides to their leaves and air movement enables us to appreciate these as they catch the sunlight.

All of the above refers to natural sunlight, but here I really want to introduce the possibility of outdoor lighting to make your garden usable at night. This is another way of adding interest to your garden without using water. It is also highly relevant, in that with the warmer summers we are experiencing there is a greater likelihood that we will have weather suitable to sit outside into the hours of darkness.

Personally adding lights to my exotic town garden in the UK immediately reminded me of holidays in faraway places with jeweled nightime gardens. Any garden centre will offer a huge array of low-voltage outdoor lights. Small spotlights are also available in sets which can be angled to light

LEFT Outdoor lighting is cheap and readily obtainable, adding a dynamic dimension to gardens for relatively little cost.

a feature, a rock or to create bold silhouette shapes from behind plants. It's very flexible and lights can easily be moved and adjusted to allow you to play with different ideas. As well those I have already mentioned there are many other options using rope lights and curtain lights to create other effects.

All garden lights, even though low-voltage, should be treated with caution. Invest in a waterproof outdoor socket, which will be wired with an RCD (residual current device) to prevent electrocution. Although electrical consumption will be very low, there are also solar powered garden lights available. Not only will these have no running costs, but they will also have no trailing cables and be totally environmentally friendly in our waterwise garden.

Even if you are unlikely to use your garden at night, it can be great fun to light it and enjoy it through the windows of your home. I have been known to turn the garden lights on in midwinter to remind myself that summer will eventually come.

Water as a garden feature

This may seem the ultimate paradox – here we are discussing waterwise gardening, where we are aiming to reduce and minimise our use of water, and I suggest using water as a feature. Most people who enjoy spending time in gardens would probably agree that water in some form is a valuable part of the landscape. Moving water is particularly appealing due to its qualities of sound and interaction with light, not to mention it's wide aesthetic appeal.

When we look at gardens through history, and in particular gardens in hot countries, we will nearly always find that water is a valuable component and sometimes quite key to such gardens. The wonderful historic gardens of Italy are full of reflecting pools and dramatic fountains. Las Vegas, set in the middle of the Nevada desert, has a string of hotels, many with huge water features such as the spectacular fountains of Bellagio. Water features not only give a cooling effect in hot climates but also demonstrate the affluence of the owners who can afford to have water in an area where it is scarce.

It is natural for gardeners to want to include water in some form in an otherwise arid and possibly desert-style garden. I have already mentioned the possibility of having a garden pool to act as a winter reservoir for irrigation and to provide water for use in the hot dry summer months, and here I want to suggest some of the more conservative forms of water features you may like to incorporate into your waterwise garden.

LEFT Simple bubble fountains such as these bamboos set in cobbles can be easily installed and use very little electricity or water.

Waterwise fountains

Elaborate and expensive water features are readily available from most garden centres. Equally, a simple fountain can be created by constructing an underground reservoir containing a small volume of water and a submersible pump. This can be topped with a mesh framework which is covered with cobbles or boulders. The fountain emerges from the stones and the trickling water drops back over the rocks and into the reservoir. Such a feature will give the sound of water with relatively little use and loss of water due to the reservoir being underground and therefore less subject to evaporation. Kits including all the components of such a feature are available from most garden centres, or you could try looking at kits sold by online retailers.

The most spectacular version of this type of waterwise fountain I have seen was in a New Zealand-themed garden designed to mimic a natural geyser. The principle was exactly the same as I have just described but the jets were set among large round boulders. The pumps were on a time switch and every few minutes a huge column of water shot into the air and dropped back down amongst the stones to the shock and delight of visitors. The effect was both dramatic and unexpected.

Numerous other small fountain and waterfall kits are available, many of them are purpose-made and ready to plug in. These may consist of a simple design such as a stone sphere sitting on top of a hollow stone column. The water trickles out of the top of the sphere and drops back into the reservoir with all the appropriate sounds. Others consist of stone pythoi with water trickling

ABOVE This dramatic imitation geyser is quite simply a powerful fountain set among huge boulders attached to a timer.

out. Probably the most fascinating are those that shoot a curving thread of water through the air making a complete arc which then drops back neatly into the receiving reservoir. There are many possibilities, all of which use a minimum of water.

The equipment for more elaborate features is expensive and, because of the accuracy involved, usually needs to be installed by a professional. Try looking in a local business directory or asking at garden centres to find a suitable trades person. Don't, whatever you do, attempt the installation yourself if you are unsure about the process in any way as the results could be disastrous.

Plants for the dry garden

Numerous plants are naturally able to tolerate water shortage and in some instances desert conditions. Such plants have natural adaptations which make them suitable for dry areas and the waterwise garden. These are natural survivors which can live through periods of water shortage, bounce back at the end and burst into growth. Drought-tolerant plants are defined as xerophytes and waterwise gardening is sometimes called xeriscaping.

Plant adaptations

Often a plant's leaves adapt to prevent it from losing excess water in hot dry spells. Succulent plants are the obvious examples of this. Not only do they have their own store of water within their fleshy leaves and stems but their surface is often waxy to prevent too much water loss. Cacti are in this group too, as they have the ability to store water. When water is freely available they take it in and retain it within their fleshy structures for use when conditions become dry. They could be described as the camels of the plant kingdom.

The presence of silver or blue/grey foliage is a good indication of a plant's ability to withstand drought, although this ability may vary in a number of ways. Initially, the pale colour reflects the light, keeping the leaf cooler and reducing the loss of water by transpiration. Some grey-leaved plants such as *Senecio cineraria* may also have fine hairs and this helps to keep the leaf temperature stable and reduce water loss. In others, the foliage is more of a blue-grey colour and this is called glaucous. Eucalyptus is an example of this with foliage that has a protective waxy deposit to slow water loss.

Leaves can be modified in other ways. Cytisus, better know as broom, has tiny leaves which lose very little water. The plant compensates for growth with green stems that are able to carry out photosynthesis. Some plants have trailing leaves to reduce the area exposed to the sun and others have waxy foliage. On other plants the stomata on their leaves is deeply sunken to reduce transpiration.

Some succulent plants also have spines and plants like Agave and some Yuccas are well equipped with vicious spikes at the end of their leaves. This is to protect them from being eaten by desert animals in search of water. If you plant these in your garden take care when working around plants with vicious spines such as this. If small children are likely to use the garden it is wise to remove the spines, which can cause serious eye injuries.

Although mostly hidden, roots are vitally important to all plants. Desert plants may have either very shallow root systems, so they can make use of what little rain reaches the surface, or may have very deep root systems so that they can search for water in deeply-seated storage areas. Many desert plants also have root systems that are adapted to store water or draw up water from deeper levels. Sometimes this takes the form of a thick fleshy tap root which penetrates deep in the soil in search of water and then stores it. This will also store food to carry the plant through difficult times.

Other plants that produce bulbs, corms and tubers go even further in their self protection. During hot dry weather they become totally dormant and all top growth dies. The plant is then able to survive on its stored resources underground until conditions are more suitable for it to grow again. Spring-flowering bulbs such as daffodils, tulips and crocus are prime examples of this. It may be a surprise to learn that plants which have traditionally been part of the garden scene in cooler climates, such as tulips, originate from hot dry areas in parts of Asia, Europe and the Middle East.

Life cycles

Many plants live for several seasons, and sometimes for many years, and so are called perennials. Many of the modifications we have described allow them to survive through testing conditions and into the following years. Annuals grow, flower and produce seeds all within one season and this is another way that some fast growing plants survive through drought. Seeds are tiny but immensely tough structures that remain alive but dormant until conditions allow them to grow.

In the extremes of hot desert conditions, such as the Cape area of South Africa, southern Australia and hot Mediterranean countries, annuals will germinate during the cool moist spring months, grow, flower and set seed before the summer droughts set in. We can learn from this survival technique and select plants more likely to thrive in hot dry conditions.

BELOW Silver foliage plants provide a very restful muted colour scheme which could be enhanced with carefully placed spots of colour.

Waterwise planting schemes

Arranging plants to be aesthetically pleasing is a matter of personal taste. Many European gardens have developed with a range of time-honoured features including lawns, borders and flower beds in styles both traditional and modern and using a wide range of plants that have hitherto been successful in other parts of the world. As we plan the waterwise garden, our choice of plants is likely to suggest other less traditional styles.

It never works to totally compartmentalize anything as subjective as garden design, so the following information can only be considered as style suggestions. As we plan a garden, we are likely to begin with a certain preconceived idea but this is likely to change and develop as both the design and eventually the landscape develops. What may start off as a gravel garden may end up as a full-blown desert garden. The main aims should be that the finished result looks good, gives pleasure to the creators and provides a successful environment for growing plants. If the end result is attractive and successful, it isn't necessary to be able to categorize it – just enjoy it.

Gravel gardens

The origin of many successful gravel gardens lies within the basics of need. When faced with inhospitable situations such as dry stony soil and low rainfall, you have two options. You can either set about the expensive and time-consuming option of trying to alter those conditions with massive soil modifications and the installation of extensive irrigation, or you could opt to work with the prevailing conditions. This is exactly what the creators of successful gravel gardens have done.

Constructing a gravel garden

Preparation for a garden is as important as for any other area or garden type. Deep cultivation should take place to break-up compacted soils and increase natural drainage followed by the incorporation of generous amounts of organic matter. Plants may well have to put up with spartan conditions once established, but giving a good, well prepared soil for initial establishment is bound to get the project off to a flying start.

It is likely that the whole surface of a gravel garden will eventually be surfaced with gravel – both your footpaths and the areas where your plants are growing. Good drainage is essential for your footpaths as well as your planted areas. Whatever rainfall there is will need to percolate, rather than sit on the surface in muddy puddles. However we will not need to incorporate organic matter in the path areas. Better to concentrate it all in the areas for planting.

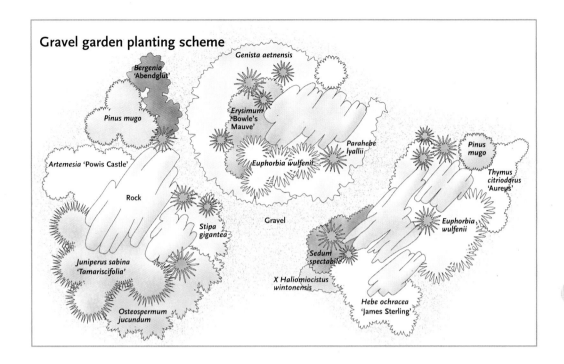

Gravel garden planting scheme

- Bergenia 'Abendglut'
- Genista aetnensis
- Pinus mugo
- Erysimum 'Bowle's Mauve'
- Parahebe lyallii
- Pinus mugo
- Artemesia 'Powis Castle'
- Euphorbia wulfenii
- Thymus citriodorus 'Aureus'
- Rock
- Gravel
- Euphorbia wulfenii
- Stipa gigantea
- Juniperus sabina 'Tamariscifolia'
- Sedum spectabile
- X Haliomiocistus wintonensis
- Osteospermum jucundum
- Hebe ochracea 'James Sterling'

Gravel gardens can be planted with or without a membrane under the gravel. Planting is easier without a membrane as you do not have to cut through the fabric; just dig a hole and plant. With later editions, you merely scrape back the surface gravel and add your extra plants. As the garden develops, plants will naturally seed and regenerate, which will result in a more natural and fully furnished effect. However as well as desirable plants there will be weeds to contend with. Without a membrane, worms will bring soil to the surface and the gravel becomes mixed with soil. After a period of a few years it will be necessary to top-up the gravel with a fresh layer.

For a really low maintenance gravel garden a sheet membrane can be placed before any planting takes place and this can go over both paths and planted areas. There are several advantages to this technique. Throughout the garden there will be less weed growth as there will be a double mulch to deter weed seedlings and retain moisture. There is also the advantage that the gravel will not disappear into the soil beneath, which is otherwise inevitable as the garden is cultivated and paths walked on.

If you opt to use a mulch fabric in your construction, this should be laid down after cultivation and before planting. In the short term it can be held down by bricks or other heavy objects to avoid it blowing away during construction. Special pins are also available for permanently holding down mulch fabric but these should not be generally necessary as you are covering this with gravel. Where sheets are joined, ensure an overlap of at least 20 cm (9 in). The fabric has the inevitable tendency to move as you work on it and gaps can easily be created. Joins are one area where pins are quite useful to anchor down permanently. It

Beth Chatto's dry garden

East Anglia is one of the driest areas of the UK, with a scant 60 cm (24 in) of rain a year. Not surprisingly it has two of the most successful dry gardens. One of these was created by Beth Chatto, whose garden at White Barn has been developing since 1960. Faced with low rainfall and areas of dry stony soil, she has spent years studying and collecting plants that naturally grow in such demanding conditions. The dry garden was developed in an area that had been a rough car park for years so it was parched, stony and compacted. In 1991 it was converted into a series of display beds where a host of differing plants all grow and thrive totally without additional irrigation. Beth's dry garden is flat with broad sweeping gravel paths and irregular shaped beds of planting.

More recently Beth has constructed a scree garden. A natural scree would be an area of loose rock that has tumbled down a mountain side during various landslides and weathering processes. In the garden a scree is usually a feature in a rock garden where plants are displayed amongst small pieces of rock and gravel. Beth's scree was built to provide an area for some of the smaller scale plants that were getting smothered in the main dry garden. Just goes to show that even with restricted water some plants can grow vigorously.

At nearby Hyde Hall, owned by the UK's Royal Horticultural Society, there is another dry garden, this time created in 2001. It displays some 730 species of plants chosen for their tolerance to drought, exposure and high light levels – along with garden worthiness. Many of the principles of construction are similar to the dry garden at White Barn but here the area slopes and different levels have been created by the use of large blocks of gabbro, an igneous rock.

Both of these gardens exhibit an amazing lushness and vigour of plant growth despite the rigid regime in which they are situated. Beth's philosophy sums up dry gardening perfectly; – 'If you choose plants adapted by nature to the conditions you have to offer, they will do well and the garden will give you a sense of peace and fulfilment.'

LEFT *Bergenias*, flowering in late summer, alongside *Sedum* and the spiky exotic foliage of an *Agave* in Beth Chatto's dry garden.

also spoils the appearance of the end result if the edges of black or white fabric appear waving in the air where the gravel has become disturbed.

Having laid your fabric, you can mark out planting areas and paths easily with a can of coloured spray paint then stand back and survey the end result before planting takes place. Lay out your plants in their pots and juggle them around until you are satisfied with the final layout and arrangement. Try to imagine how the plants will look when they have grown to their full height and spread. The individual planting position for each plant should then be cut-out using a sharp knife to cut a cross in the fabric. Fold back the fabric, dig a suitable sized hole, plant to the right depth, firm and then fold back the four corners of the fabric around the plant. The better protected the soil, the less chance of weed

ABOVE This *Euphorbia*, with grasses and phormiums, provides interest in the gravel garden, even in the depths of winter.

growth. You can also do this job with many fabrics by burning out a hole with a blow torch. Most mulch fabrics are plastic-based and applying heat causes the material to melt leaving a round hole that will not fray. It's certainly neater but there are some safety risks in using a blow torch and, in my opinion, the smaller hole makes planting more difficult.

Finish off your gravel garden with a good 5 cm (2 in) layer of gravel. A locally quarried pea shingle is undoubtedly going to be the cheapest material but there will be numerous other alternatives. Golden gravel looks very attractive, as do red or green chippings. Alternatively slate can be used. Many different effects can be created and there is no reason why you cannot use more than one material. You might possibly wish to use one material

ABOVE There's nothing boring about this desert-style garden with its towering grasses and spikey succulents, set against a lone pine.

for your paths and a contrasting aggregate for the planted areas. Remember, loose materials will inevitably kick around and after a time the contrast will become indistinct as the materials mix.

Creating a desert garden

Most gardens are really horticultural theatre and so we choose those elements that we like and features that we feel will add to the atmosphere, but they will rarely be realistic. True deserts are bleak, stark places, and although they may certainly have areas of botanical interest, they are unlikely to be friendly welcoming places.

A desert garden is similar to a gravel garden but usually more sparse with less plants and more open space. Most desert gardens are very simple in style consisting of sweeping undulations of fine sand or soil with widely spaced, striking specimen plants. The desert-style gardens we create will include many plants that grow in desert regions and will have elements from reality too, but these will be highly sanitized to make them appealing.

The floor of your desert garden will probably be composed of sand or fine gravel – whatever is readily and cheaply available in your area. Some such aggregates will be more attractive than others. If you are lucky enough to live an area where the natural stone is an attractive colour or is of volcanic derivation, this is likely to provide a good desert floor. Such an aggre-

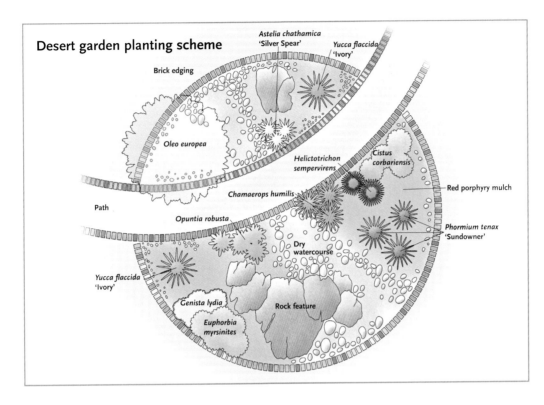

Desert garden planting scheme

- Astelia chathamica 'Silver Spear'
- Yucca flaccida 'Ivory'
- Brick edging
- Oleo europea
- Helictotrichon sempervirens
- Cistus corbariensis
- Red porphyry mulch
- Chamaerops humilis
- Path
- Opuntia robusta
- Phormium tenax 'Sundowner'
- Yucca flaccida 'Ivory'
- Dry watercourse
- Genista lydia
- Rock feature
- Euphorbia myrsinites

gate will make a fine pleasing mulch, both orna-mental and effective.

Although the floor of your desert can be flat, it is likely to be more effective if it is created with gentle sweeping undulations. Build-up the basic contours using the garden soil before you plant and finish with the mulch. Remember that there is nothing to hold the mulch in place so contours should be gentle. Round aggregates such as small pebbles will roll down any steep slopes. The aggregate can be in different sizes for added interest or one fine grade which can be raked for a very stark stylized finish.

Using rock

Rocks are often included in desert landscapes. These should ideally be larger pieces of the same stone from which your surface aggregate is derived. Choose some really nice pieces, as big as you can handle, but remember stone is very heavy and if not moved with great care could cause a serious injury. Most quarries will let you choose pieces yourself so it is worth having some idea in advance as to whether you want smooth round boulders, long low pieces or thin slivers that can be installed as upright sentinels.

In general fewer large pieces of stone will be far more effective than a greater quantity of small pieces. Remember this is a desert, not a rock garden. Positioning of stone will often be linked with planting and as you won't want to be moving stone around a great deal, try to imagine it in its final position or make a sketch to work out the most attractive arrangement.

ABOVE A single rock, a spiky plant and a red gravel mulch, enriched by the fleeting shadow patterns on a sunny day.

Always wear leather gloves when handling large stones and boots with steel toe caps. Try to lever or roll rocks and only lift the smaller pieces. A sack barrow may be useful for moving stones any distance but beware that the wheels don't slip into a soft patch and discharge your rocks in totally the wrong place. Planks may be useful for sliding stones into tricky positions. A good proportion of any stone should always be buried in the ground. This helps the stone to look natural and also gives it stability. Any tall upright stones should particularly be well anchored in the ground to avoid them coming loose and being a safety risk. It might be a good idea to concreted big tall stones in place to avoid any accidents. This is particularly important in any garden used by children who might climb on stone features.

Arranging the plants

The plants chosen for a desert garden should generally be large substantial specimens. This is one garden style where less is definitely more. Big advanced plants are always more expensive, but if you are buying just a few big plants for an area rather than dozens of smaller plants it is likely that the overall cost will not be much more. Choose your plants carefully, selecting those with good shapes and with a range of heights; low chunky plants, spiky ones and tall thin specimens. Sometimes a less than perfect plant with an odd shape may be just the thing to plant alongside a piece of oddly-shaped stone. Try to think of the end result in terms of the whole composition.

In a desert garden the space in between the plants and rocks is as important as the components of the landscape. This will enable you to see the full shape of individual plants or the combined shape of an arrangement of rocks and plants, and often from different angles. These should be a series of small features within the clear floorscape between. Such space will also give room for shadows. Bright light casts strong shadows and these can be a valuable but constantly changing part of the composition.

Mediterranean gardens

A Mediterranean garden may have a certain style but, more than anything else, it is a garden that is ruled by the prevailing weather. It will be comprised of plants that grow and thrive in hot dry summers followed by mild wet winters. A Mediterranean gardener is no more or less than a waterwise gardener. Both gardening styles involve an understanding of the basic principles and a respect for concepts like autumn planting, allowing new plants to establish a good root system before the rigours of a hot summer.

A good, well-planned Mediterranean garden can look lush and very green despite low rainfall and very limited irrigation. This is in part due to good plant selection. It is also true that good thick planting will conserve water and reduce temperatures. Dense groundcover plantings will cover the soil, keeping it cool and reducing water loss. A spreading tree will also produce shade, lower the temperature thereby conserve moisture.

Plants within a Mediterranean climate may behave differently to their counterparts in more temperate areas. Species may flower earlier or remain evergreen rather than shedding their leaves in winter. As I write this,

following record UK temperatures in April, at the Chelsea flower show in London exhibitors are bemoaning the fact that many of their selected plants have come into flower early and will be useless for the show. We have a learning curve here.

Even if the opportunity to garden near the Mediterranean Sea seems remote, you may like the challenge of creating a garden with a Mediterranean feel. Initially the aim is to create an atmosphere – a quiet, peaceful, relaxed feeling, redolent of warm summer days with nothing better to do than meander in a pleasant garden.

BELOW Most Mediterranean gardens have a green lushness that often hides the warm dry conditions in which they grow and thrive.

Mediterranean garden planting scheme

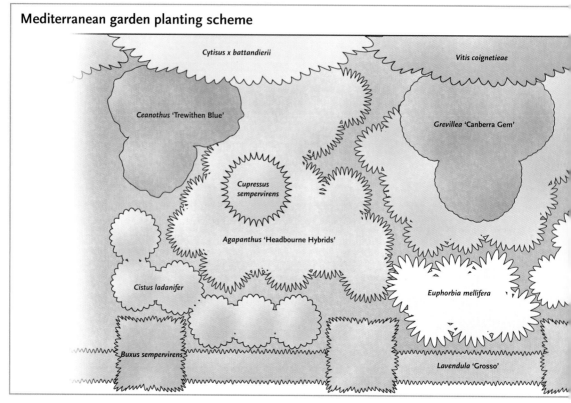

Cytisus x battandierii

Vitis coignetieae

Ceanothus 'Trewithen Blue'

Grevillea 'Canberra Gem'

Cupressus
sempervirens

Agapanthus 'Headbourne Hybrids'

Cistus ladanifer

Euphorbia mellifera

Buxus sempervirens

Lavendula 'Grosso'

Creating the effect

Most good Mediterranean gardens have a
sense of antiquity about them, given by old
buildings, stonework, steps and terraces.
This may not be easy in the surroundings of
a small modern garden. Builders' salvage
yards are marvellous places to acquire bits of
old architecture, sections of demolished
pillars, pieces of carved stone, tiles, bricks,
even old statues and gates. This is the best
way of getting a pseudo-classical feel. Some
suppliers also produce modern reproduc-
tions of classical urns and so on but these
can be expensive and slow to weather. Also

RIGHT The remains of the old Abbey in Tresco gardens give
the prefect setting for this Mediterranean garden, here with a
bold clump of agapanthus in the foreground.

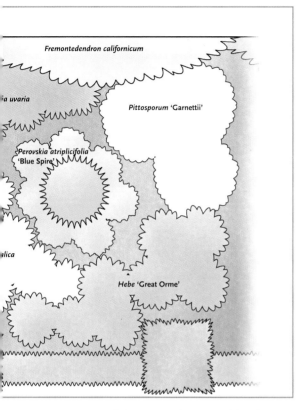

Fremontedendron californicum

...ia uvaria

Pittosporum 'Garnettii'

Perovskia atriplicifolia 'Blue Spire'

...alica

Hebe 'Great Orme'

and pergolas that create overhead shade with climbers is another constituent. Vines are a must and you can either choose a fruiting type or quite simply *Vitis coignetiae* for its huge leaves and glowing autumn tints. Try to add some real exotics that would be seen nowhere except in a Mediterranean garden. Plants like pink Bougainvillea, blue Plumbago, passion flowers and maybe some Citrus work well. All will be tender and need the protection from frost but they can be wheeled-out in pots for summer interest.

Terracotta pots seem to be another feature of the dream Mediterranean garden. Lots of them in untidy groups, different sizes and shapes with lots of exuberant plants, ivy-leaved pelargoniums, agapanthus, and of course succulents such as the spiky Agave. Ornamental urns and troughs can be planted in a similar way. Alternatively classical pithoi and the like will stand on their own as a feature without any planting.

Many Mediterranean gardens will be formal with straight paths of gravel or deco-rative paving and geometrically shaped beds and borders. These are often edged with lavender or clipped box, another important Mediterranean plant. Alongside this formality there will also be a sort of rugged exuberance from the tumbling climbers and overflowing plant pots.

Finally, the Mediterranean garden must have water in some form. This can take the form of a large pool with fountain or a simple small jet that trickles water into a wall basin. Either will work well.

Add together at least a few of the above constituents and you stand a fair chance of creating at least a touch of the Mediterranean.

never regard slopes or changes of level as problems but use them to provide interest in a garden.

The plants in a Mediterranean garden can be widely selected, but you should try to includes some pencil-thin cypresses, palms, spiky plants such as Yuccas and an olive tree. The latter can be bought as either a young plant, with no character, or as an older plant which will already be gnarled and twisted. Such specimens may be costly. If you have the space an evergreen oak is another good constituent. Aromatic plants such as lavender, thyme and sage will also be impor-tant and add interest.

Don't forget that shade is an important part of a Mediterranean garden, so trellises

Derek Jarman's seaside garden

This garden is somewhat unique. Few knowledgeable gardener's would dream of trying to create a garden under the conditions in which Derek created his seaside garden. Derek was an artist, film-maker and theatrical designer. He lived in a small wooden chalet on the shingle beach within sight of Dungeness nuclear power station, on the windy Kent coast in England. The garden he created here had to cope with not only very dry conditions but also wind, lack of real soil and salt spray. Yet despite this and maybe partly because of this, Derek created a small paradise garden that expressed his pioneering and artistic personality.

Derek's garden is full of 'things'! Mainly things washed up by the tide, which others might regard as junk but which provided Derek

with numerous natural sculptures with which to create his garden. Here you will find driftwood in every shape and size, from tall geometric pieces of wood shaped in the past to some purpose but softened by the sea and time. Alongside these are pieces of natural driftwood and roots from trees, originally living entities, once growing on some far flung shore. Metal is present, often rusted and twisted and sometimes formed into new compositions such as a sculpture from old garden tools. There is even an old upturned galvanised water tank acting as a display table for flints and stones and surrounded by red poppies. Stones, rocks and cobbles are selected and arranged everywhere.

Alongside all these inanimate objects there are more living, thriving plants than you would ever imagine in such a hostile situation. Silvery foliage such as Santolina, Helichryssum and cardoons thrive alongside the more colourful Californian poppies, valerian and pot marigolds. The inevitable Seakale is there with other natives such as dog rose and gorse. Pink hollyhocks, orange wallflowers and purple honesty give us a touch of the cottage garden, but certainly not in a traditional sense. Slightly more exotic plants such as Cistus, Yucca, lavender and iris are there. Adding the overtones of scent we have herbs such as rosemary, fennel, mint, thyme, sage, rue and a host more mingling with the robust smell of the sea. Derek despised formal gardens and so everything is naturally ragged but nevertheless formed and designed.

LEFT This strange but beautiful garden shows the defiance of plants thriving even in the most inhospitable of conditions.

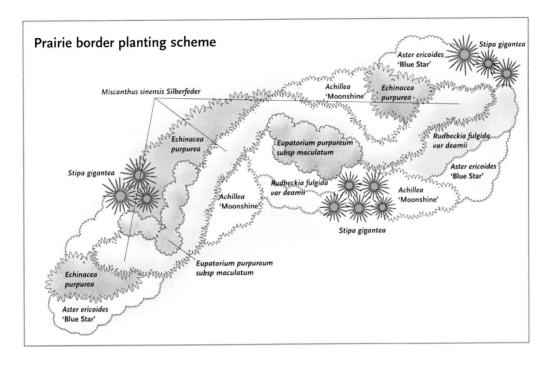

Prairie border planting scheme

Stipa gigantea

Aster ericoides 'Blue Star'

Miscanthus sinensis Silberfeder

Echinacea purpurea

Achillea 'Moonshine'

Echinacea purpurea

Rudbeckia fulgida var deamii

Stipa gigantea

Eupatorium purpureum subsp maculatum

Aster ericoides 'Blue Star'

Echinacea purpurea

Rudbeckia fulgida var deamii

Achillea 'Moonshine'

Achillea 'Moonshine'

Stipa gigantea

Eupatorium purpureum subsp maculatum

Echinacea purpurea

Aster ericoides 'Blue Star'

Prairie gardens

Natural prairies are mixed grasslands generally found in areas of North America. The dominant vegetation is grass with other wild herbaceous plants, sometimes with small shrubs and occasional trees. Prairies are generally in areas where a temperate climate prevails but are often subject to severe summer drought. Plant species in a prairie have evolved to survive in these extreme conditions.

This natural vegetation type has been used as a model for a landscape-style that has become popular in recent years. It has been particularly developed in Europe by designers such as Piet Oudolf. Ornamental grasses are planted together with herbaceous perennials and sometimes bulbs and small shrubs in large, informal swathes and drifts. The aim is to emulate the natural prairies using a wider mix of cultivated plants. Depending on the space avail-

able you can use short compact grasses and perennials or big vigorous spreading types.

Prairie planting is based on ecological principles of plant community and sustainability, but it is not a natural planting and does not primarily use native species. The aim is to create a highly colourful and dramatic swathe of vegetation that has a long season of interest, is cheap to establish and has low maintenance. By using exotic and attractive species and cultivars, a high level of interest can be created.

A prairie garden should not be confused with a herbaceous border or even an island bed; the effect must be looser and more natural. Perennials chosen should be self-supporting – you don't want to have to use stakes and ties which would spoil the relaxed effect. Although there will probably be a high proportion of grasses, this is also not the same as a wildflower meadow, which will have more native species.

A wild prairie is often very much of a single height with daisies and other flowers hovering amongst the grasses. A gardener designing a prairie planting will take this a stage further by choosing species that will produce big bold shapes that will grow out above the rest of the planting. This may result in swathes of ornamental grasses with big clumps of Eupatorium, Thalictrum or Rudbeckia bursting through. Prairies generally do not have colour schemes, although there is no reason why there shouldn't be one. They tend to be planned to peak in late summer. This will be the time when many of the grasses will be at their best, so by choosing herbaceous perennials such as Aster, Helenium, Echinacea and Rudbeckia you will have a range of flowers amongst the grasses.

Planting a prairie

Prairie plantings look best in as large a space as possible. Don't just put a small bed in the middle of the lawn, but replace the lawn completely with a prairie planting with paths winding through so the effect can be experienced at close quarters. Prairies are generally informal but notable ones have been created at Wisley and at Trentham Gardens in the UK, and these both have geometric beds as their location.

Prepare the area for a prairie planting by cultivating as normal. Most grasses and the other plants you will be using do not require a rich soil so additional organic matter is not needed, unless the soil is very poor and dry. It is helpful to make sure that the area is free from perennial weeds so advance preparation followed by a treatment with glyphosate is valuable to control any 'nasties' that emerge.

Grasses are generally best planted in early-to mid-spring, and this is fine too for most peren-

nials. Although we have elsewhere recommended autumn planting this is not good for grasses which are likely to fail if the winter is wet. Plants are generally spaced about 30-45 cm (12-18 in) apart. The whole arrangement can be very relaxed and loose with plants generally scattered and mixed throughout the area. However you may wish to locate groups of key statement plants, the ones with height and good shapes, in prominent positions. If using in groups, remember threes, fives, sevens and so on always look good for plant groups.

A prairie planting can be established through a membrane like our gravel garden, although here you will be wanting to positively encourage seeding of grasses and other species to enhance the natural effect. A membrane will prevent this happening. Here it will be better to use a mulch of bark or even gravel. Some weeding may be needed with a new prairie plantings but once established the plants should almost look after themselves. Some weed will hardly show amongst other vigorous planting.

At the end of the summer, much of the planting can be left untouched overwinter for its architectural effect. Grasses nearly always look good as dormant skeletons and the seedheads of many herbaceous perennials will often have a winter presence, all enhanced by frost! In the spring the whole area can be cut down using a mower set high or a strimmer. If using a mower the resulting trimmings can probably be left as a mulch, otherwise it must be raked off. Some gardeners will recommend burning off a prairie planting every few years but this is a risky proposition unless you know exactly what you are doing.

RIGHT Many prairie plantings, such as this mix of *Heleniums, Echinacea* and ornamental grasses, are at their best in late summer.

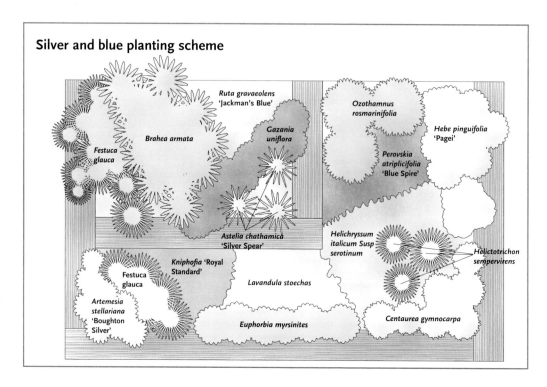

Silver and blue planting scheme

Festuca glauca

Brahea armata

Ruta gravaeolens 'Jackman's Blue'

Gazania uniflora

Ozothamnus rosmarinifolia

Hebe pinguifolia 'Pagei'

Perovskia atriplicifolia 'Blue Spire'

Astelia chathamica 'Silver Spear'

Helichryssum italicum Susp serotinum

Helictotrichon sempervirens

Festuca glauca

Kniphofia 'Royal Standard'

Lavandula stoechas

Artemesia stellariana 'Boughton Silver'

Euphorbia myrsinites

Centaurea gymnocarpa

Silver and blue gardens

Silver plants achieved a certain fashion in the 1970s. In the UK Mrs Desmond Underwood published a book on *Grey & Silver Plants*, which was linked to her nursery specializing in these plants. Kew Gardens just outside London also had a silver garden for many years around the Wood Museum. Like many fashions, it drifted away and silver borders are rarely regarded as fashionably acceptable...

Having said that there is an amazing array of different types of foliage and plants with different habits amongst silver foliage plants. From the smallest of prostrate *Artemesia stellariana* 'Boughton Silver' at a mere 5 cm (2 in) up to the tree proportions of *Eucalyptus gunni* at 25 m (80 ft). The relevance to the waterwise garden is that silver foliage plants are, in general, very tolerant of low water regimes. Some, such

as the eucalypts, have very waxy surfaces and these tend to be the ones with a bluish tinge, whereas others, for example *Verbascum* 'Arctic Silver', have a whitish colouring which is caused by a covering of fine hairs over the surface of the leaf. Both are means by which the leaf prevents excess water loss.

Quite a few grasses are silvery-blue in colour and and these would fit well in this garden. The delicate vertical foliage contrasts well with other leaf formations. Possible candidates would include *Festuca* 'Blue Elijah' , *Koeleria glauca*, *Leymus arenarius* and *Helictotrichon sempervirons*. All are excellent drought tolerant grasses.

Silver foliage plants are valuable constituents of any waterwise planting scheme and should not be overlooked. Using them as a theme should also not be dismissed but I would suggest that combining them with other colours is the most effective way to use them. So many ideas in the garden are re-inventions of past styles or fashions with a new twist. For example a sea of differing silver foliage could be punctuated by strong colours such as the striking orange of *Kniphofias*, Californian poppies or *Crocosmia*.

There are also an astounding number of plants with almost black foliage, such as *Ophiopogon planiscapus* 'Nigrescens', *Aeonium arboretum* 'Schwarzkopf' or *Phormium* 'Platt's Black'. Even with the restrictions of low water, there are still many to choose from. Black and silver is a classic scheme and will always look startling, possibly with the addition of white flowers or the use of a highlight colour such as red or orange. Finding plants that will grow successfully and fit the narrow narrow criteria of this scheme may be a challenge, but the end result will certainly be worth the effort.

BELOW A silver and blue scheme using blue petunias softened with *Calocephalus brownii*, the 'wire wool' plant, and spiky *Leymus arenarius*.

A-Z of Waterwise Plants

Survivors and thrivers

The following is a list of plants suggested for the waterwise garden. I have tried where possible to indicate those that *thrive* in dry conditions and those that *survive* despite dry conditions, although they might prefer more water. This is a very imprecise distinction and will be dependent on the severity of the drought and the temperatures prevailing. A great deal of gardening is trial and error and part of the fun is the successes we achieve often unexpectedly.

Hardiness and zoning

Over recent years, gardeners have become more adventurous. Plants from many Mediterranean areas such as South Africa, California, Australia, New Zealand and even South America have appeared in our garden centres and become surprisingly comfortable in our gardens. With fewer frosts and generally higher winter temperatures we can afford to be adventurous in our planting. Many of these plants from Mediterranean areas are ideal for our waterwise garden.

Within our A-Z of waterwise plants you will see Z symbols with a number after most plant listings. These refer to a hardiness system developed in the USA and based on an annual minimum temperatures for certain areas. Plants are rated with the lowest zone in which they are likely to survive. So if a plant is listed as a Z8 plant it is likely also to survive in Z9 but not Z7 or lower. In the past it has not been widely used in the UK but you may find references to this system in parts of Europe. Being a small island the UK does not have great differences of climate and generally lies between zones 7 to 9 with the majority of the country being Z8.

As well as the hotter summers, many temperate areas have been experiencing milder winters and less frost, so it is worth considering those that are on the borderline for our area, particularly Z9 plants. Gardeners in many areas have discovered that they can grow and overwinter plants that would never have seemed hardy twenty years ago. This is one of the exciting aspects of global warming and offers us a whole host of new plants that gardeners would never dreamed of growing outdoors in the past. In the following list there will be a number of plants noted as being borderline hardiness. These are the gambles. All adventurous gardeners are horticultural speculators and love the challenge of trying something new. Some may not be successful but others will be and may well end up becoming a regular part of our gardens and landscapes in the future.

RIGHT The Mexican Blue palm, *Brahea armata*, is an expensive gamble but a wonderful plant that may well survive in a sheltered spot.

Acacia

Leguminosae

A large genus but generally widely recognized as the fluffy bobbly yellow flowers called mimosa, often seen as cut flower in florist shops in the spring, *A. dealbata* (Z9) silver wattle is easily grown and proving to be hardy in many locations, although it originates from Australia. The foliage is silver and finely divided. Grow it against a warm wall or in the open as a tree. If it gets too big it can be cut down and allowed to regenerate as a multi-stemmed plant. It needs full sun and a well-drained site.

Acanthus

Acanthaceae

This genus of herbaceous perennials is recognized by many as the leaf has been used as a motif in architecture since ancient Greek culture. It is a tough herbaceous perennial with deeply cut dark green leaves. The striking flowers are arranged around a tall stem. Individual white flowers are hooded with purple and the whole structure is prickly so handle carefully. *A. mollis* (Z7) is the commonest but *A. spinosus* (Z7) is more delicate with finely cut foliage, both growing to about 90 cm(3 ft) in height. Grows in sun or shade and is reasonably drought tolerant.

Acca *(syn Feijoa)*

Myrtaceae

A small genus from sub-tropical South America but proving quite tough and hardy in many gardens. Makes a compact bush with green leaves with silvery undersides. *A. sellowiana* (Z8) produces small red and white flowers with fluffy orange stamens. In warm climates it produces edible fruits known as pineapple guavas. It is said to have been Queen Victoria of England's favourite fruit. There is a variegated form which is slightly less hardy but very attractive. Both are evergreen.

Achillea

Asteraceae/Compositae

These herbaceous perennials are the cultivated forms of the white wild flower known as yarrow. For many years the most familiar was a tall and coarse yellow sold as *A. filipendulina* 'Gold Plate' (Z3). The shorter and paler *A. millefolium* 'Moonshine' (Z2) is much more refined in primrose yellow and very free flowering.

In recent years plant breeders have produced a whole kaleidoscope of new cultivars with compact habits such as 'Cerise Queen', dark pink, 'Fanal' red, 'Paprika', orange, 'Lilac Beauty' and lavender. Most are less than 90 cm (3 ft) in height. *A. ptarmica* 'the Pearl' (Z5) is a low-growing cultivar with small double button-like white blooms, very much a cottage garden plant. All are tolerant of reasonably dry conditions.

Aeonium

Crassulaceae

Coming from the Canary Isles, North Africa and the Mediterranean, these succulent sub shrubs are tender. Most people would recognise the familiar *A. arboreum* AGM (Z9) as a dusty houseplant that seems to thrive on neglect. The dark leaved form known as 'Schwarzkopf' AGM (Z9) is a spectacular plant with rosettes of rich purple, almost black foliage. They need to be grown in very well drained gritty compost and because they are tender are best considered as pot plants that can be brought outside for the summer and taken indoors for the winter.

Agapanthus

Alliaceae/Liliaceae

These wonderful South African herbaceous perennials give a very welcome burst of blue flowers in midsummer. All have strap-like leaves and generally the deciduous types are the hardier hybrids as opposed the species, which are evergreen but often tender. The flowers are borne as umbels at the top of a slender stem up to about 90 cm (3 ft) in height.

One of the most familiar hardy types is the 'Headbourne Hybrids' (Z7). These are a rather vague group of plants grown from seed. Although hardy and often attractive they can be very variable. There are many different named cultivars including whites and shades of blue through to deep indigo. These all thrive in well drained hot sunny positions.

Agave

Agavaceae

This is a genus of succulent and generally spikey-leaved plants from North, Central and Southern America. They are half hardy or frost tender but with our increasingly mild winters, will sometimes survive outdoors in sheltered and very well drained spots. Alternatively grow them in pots and take into a frost-free greenhouse for the winter. Most produce a spiky rosette of very rigid foliage, often topped with lethal spines. They are most strikingly architectural plants and perfect for a desert style garden or as potted specimens. The most familiar and easily grown is the plain green,

BELOW Blue flowers, such as these giant headed *Agapanthus*, are a welcome contrast in any garden and very tolerant of dry conditions.

waxy-leaved *A. americana*, AGM (Z9). Its varie-gated forms are certainly more interesting but undoubtedly more tender. All need very well drained soil in a hot sunny spot.

Allium

Liliaceae

This is the onion family and as well as the edible types, there are hundreds of different ornamental species with beautiful flowers and often attractive seed heads which retain their structure and beauty right through the winter. In general they are hardy bulbous plants that come from dry mountainous areas. Most flower in spring or early summer and then go dormant over the hot dry summer months so they are ideally adapted to the dry garden. Most can be easily propagated from seeds and in situations such as gravel gardens, they will seed and naturally spread on their own. Like many bulbs, they are good filler plants that can be interplanted between other things for extra interest and to give stunning two layer effects.

There are many good garden types to choose from so I am suggesting just a few favourites. *A cernuum*, AGM (Z3) (the 'nodding onion') grows to about 45 cm (18 in) with delicate heads of pendent pink flowers. *A cristophii*, AGM, syn *A. albopilosum*, produces stems up to 60 cm (2 ft) with huge circular heads about 20 cm (8 in) across bearing masses of tiny pink starry flowers. The seed-heads dry well and last a long time. *A. flavum* AGM (Z3), and *A. moly* AGM, known as the golden garlic, are both short plants with yellow flowers, and *A. caeruleum* is a tall blue. And of course the common *A. schoenoprasum*, better know as chives, is both ornamental,, with pink flower heads and of great value in the kitchen.

There are so many varieties to choose from and they will also thrive in pots as well as the open border.

Alstroemeria

Alstroemeriaceae

These plants are commonly known as Peruvian lilies and mostly originate from mountain screes or dry grasslands in South America. They are often seen as multi-coloured, long-lasting cut flowers. In recent years they have been highly hybridized to produce some very colourful and low growing cultivars. These are tuberous plants which strongly resent distur-bance so plant as growing plants from pots with as little disruption as possible. Avoid dried roots, which are very likely to fail.

A. aurea, syn *A. aurantiaca* (Z7) is an unimproved species, which if established can spread and may be invasive, but in a rather nice way. It's display may be short-lived and it can be shy to flower. Much better are hybrid types such as the Ligtu hybrids or more recent Princess, Little Princess or Little Miss series. The Princess Series were bred for cut flowers so have taller stems, the others are short garden hybrids. All are free flowering with brilliant beautifully marked flowers. Nice plants to allow to ramble between other plants. Mostly Zone 7.

Anthemis

Asteraceae/Compositae

This group of plants are all simple daisies in shades of yellow, primrose and white. Most have finely cut foliage that is pungently aromatic and sometimes silvery. They like dry hot sunny locations are tolerant of water

RIGHT Plant *Agave americana* in a hot dry sunny position and it will not only survive the drought but also overwinter in all but the coldest temperatures.

shortage so ideal for our dry gardens. *A. punctata* subsp. *cupiana*, AGM (Z7) which, despite its dreadful name, is a lovely plant with a mat of silver foliage that is then topped with masses of delicate white daisies with golden centres. *A. tinctoria* 'E.C. Buxton' (Z6) is a taller herbaceous plant with slender stems growing to about 60 cm (2 ft) and bearing lemon yellow daisies. It is exceptionally free flowering through the early summer months.

Arabis

Brassicaceae/Cruciferae

These are short-lived cushion forming perennials commonly known as rock cress and often grown as rock garden plants. They are mostly white or shades of pink and flower in the spring. They are generally hybrids of *A. caucasica* (Z3) such as 'Flore Pleno' AGM which is a double white and Variegata, which has leaves with gold margins. 'Rosabella' produces pale pink flowers and 'Frühlingszauber' AGM rich cerise pink flowers. They all like the full sun and will tolerate dry poor soils. They can also be grown as plants for a spring hanging basket or container.

Armeria

Plumbaginaceae

It never fails to amaze me how seemingly dissimilar plants can be related. This insignificant tufty herbaceous plant seems such an unlikely relative for the exotic, powder blue climber Plumbago. This little native of sea cliffs and mountains is a real toughie. It has narrow,° almost grass-like foliage in small clumps and then each spring produces a mass of short stems with little pink bobbles of flowers. There are named cultivars such as 'Bee's Ruby' AGM and 'Bevan's Variety' AGM,

(both Z4). All will tolerate full sun but need a well drained situation.

Artemesia

Asteraceae/Compositae

Most of the species in this useful genus have silver foliage of some sort. There are some short-lived shrubs and others are herbaceous perennials. All need a well-drained site and are best positioned in full sun. Wet winters are inclined to damage them and prolonged wet conditions at any time of year may well reduce their life-span.

A. absinthium 'Lambrook Silver' AGM (Z5) has lovely finely divided silver foliage. The flowers that appear in mid summer are disappointing and it is best trimmed back to encourage more foliage. *A. ludoviciana* 'Silver Queen' (Z4) is another silver foliage herbaceous plant, shorter but less finely cut foliage. The cultivar A. 'Powis Castle' (Z9) is an evergreen shrub that forms a low cushion of almost white, finely dissected foliage. It is rapid growing and should be pruned hard each spring to get fresh lush foliage. With wet winters it is sadly often short-lived but is easily propagated by semi-ripe cuttings in the autumn. *A. schmidtiana* AGM makes a low tufted perennial with delicate foliage like silvery silken threads. A choice plant for a location where it can be appreciated at close-quarters. My last suggestion is a real personal favourite. *A. stelleriana* 'Boughton Silver' syn A. 'Mori', (Z4) makes a flat carpet of silver foliage with leaves almost like tiny white hands but with too many fingers. This species can look miserable in a damp winter but really comes into its own with the warm dry weather that summer (hopefully) bings. Persistence is key here.

Astelia

Asteliaceae/Liliaceae

This is a wonderful little group of evergreen perennials from Australia, New Zealand and New Guinea. Best known for *A. chathamica* 'Silver Spear' AGM, which makes a soft spiky plant – in other words with long thin leaves that gently arch. The foliage is a soft green on the upper sides and pure silver underneath giving an agreeably contrasting effect.

Opinions seem to differ about its survival in drought but I have found it to be tough and undemanding in a dry situation. There are some attractive bronze-leaved versions such as 'Westland'. These are not a deep brown, more of a gentle coppery bronze, but sufficiently different to be desirable. It is on the borderline of hardiness so needs good drainage and a sheltered site. It has proved quite hardy for several years in my Midlands garden in the UK.

Ballota

Lamiaceae

B. acetabulosa (Z8) is a useful filler or background plant that is not visually spectacular but is thoroughly reliable in dry well drained conditions. It produces vertical stems crowded with pairs of small heart-shaped leaves covered in a silvery white fur. Its tiny pinkish flowers are insignificant but leave behind an attractive papery bract. There is a plain green form called 'All Hallow's Green' with tiny greenish flowers.

BELOW As well as spring flowers, *Bergenia Ballawley* has evergreen foliage with wonderful burnished winter tints.

PLANTING IDEA

Try planting *Berberis* x *darwinii* with a purple leaved shrub such as *Cotinus coggygria* 'Atropurpurea' or *Weigelia florida* 'Foliis Purpureis'. The rich orange early summer flowers of the berberis look startling against the fresh rich purple foliage.

Berberis

Berberidaceae

This is a vast group of prickly shrubs with many species and attractive cultivars. They like full sun or partial shade and once established will tolerate a reasonable level of drought. Some people would regard these as very 'common' plants and certainly not desert species, but they are very tough and useful. They can be used as background plants or as barriers because of their prickly nature. *B. julianae* and *B. gagnepainii* both have very long sharp prickles so are best avoided in gardens with children, but of great use where a solid barrier is required for security reasons.

Many also have spectacular early summer flowers in yellow or orange, which are often followed by autumn displays of brightly coloured or black berries. *B. wilsonsoniae* has particularly attractive coral red, almost translucent berries in chunky clusters. There are many coloured leaved forms of *B. thunbergii* such as 'Dart's Red Lady' with rich ruby foliage or *B. thunbergii* 'Aurea' with gold foliage. There are evergreen forms such as *B.* x *stenophylla* AGM, which makes a good flowering hedge with arching sprays of orange flowers. Some of the deciduous types such a *B.* x *ottawensis* 'Superba' AGM provide a late display of vivid autumn colour before dropping their leaves. All round a very valuable genus of good garden plants.

Bergenia

Saxifragaceae

Known commonly as 'Elephant's Ears' because of their broad flat leaves, these easy plants are often maligned and generally loved or hated. They actually prefer moist conditions where they will thrive but are very tolerant and useful, particularly in dry shady conditions. Most are evergreen and with some such as 'Ballawley', (Z4) the foliage assumes rich ruby tones over-winter. Foliage is otherwise glossy and dark green and most are evergreen.

They generally flower in mid to late spring with flowers in varying shades of pink, rose and white. The cultivar 'Silberlicht' AGM (Z4) is a good almost pure white and at the other end of the spectrum, 'Abendglut', syn 'Evening Glow', (Z4) is a rich ruby red. *B. cordifolia* (Z3) is the commonest and toughest. The cultivar 'Tubby Andrews' is variegated with splashes of gold and pale green, which is even more attractive in winter when the leaves also assume pinkish tints.

All are hardy and suitable with the exception of *B. ciliata* (Z7) which although lovely, is not suitable for the waterwise garden as it needs a damp shady spot to thrive.

Beschorneria

Agavaceaea

Another clump-forming plant with an ever-green rosette of soft spiky foliage, originating from desert areas of Mexico. Most commonly known for the species *B. yuccoides* AGM (Z8) which not surprisingly looks for much of its life like a small greenish leaved yucca plant. However when it comes into flower it sends up

RIGHT *Astelia nervosa* 'Silver Spear' is another tough and spiky plant, this one with shiny green foliage backed with silver.

a hansome tall spike to about 1.5 m (5 ft) with spectacular greenish yellow flowers with red bracts. Quite an eye catcher. It is very much borderline hardiness so will need a very warm sheltered spot.

Brachyglottis
Asteraceae/Compositae
This is primarily included for some species that used to be in the genus Senecio but the botanists moved them and renamed them. They come from scrubby, rocky areas of New Zealand and Australia and are in general very tough and drought tolerant.

The most familiar is probably S. 'Sunshine' AGM. It is still sometimes called *S. greyii*, although this is technically just one of its parents that is rarely seen. This is the familiar grey leaved shrub that grows to around 1.2 m (4 ft) with bright yellow daisy flowers in midsummer. It has been widely overplanted and can be seen in almost any supermarket car park. However this is for good reason, as it is tough and very tolerant of all sorts of conditions including heat and drought. The closely related *S. monroi* AGM, is shorter in stature and has smaller leaves, that are finely crimped at the edges but the overall plant shape can be a bit ragged.

Buddleja *syn Buddleia*
Buddlejaceae/Loganiaceae
The familiar butterfly bush is known for its ability to colonise any bare ground, however dry and stony it may be, which makes it of particular interest to any gardener wishing to create a waterwise garden. These plants come from rocky and scrubby areas in Asia, Africa, North and South America but are nearly all very hardy. Most of the familiar

types are cultivars of *B. davidii* (Z5). They are fast growing shrubs that should be pruned hard in early spring every year but will still make 1.8 m (6 ft) growth in a season. In late summer they produce long panicles bearing myriads of tiny flowers in varying shades from white, through to pinks and blues to deep rich purples. They have a somewhat cloying fragrance, although that may be just my opinion...

'Black Knight' AGM is a very deep rich plum colour, 'White Profusion' AGM a snowy white, and 'Nanho Blue' a mid-blue on a compact bush. 'Harlequin' has yellow variegated leaves and screaming, unmissable rich purple-red flowers.

B. globosa bears round orange flowers on a big rounded bush and *B. alternifolia* (Z6) has very slender pale lavender flowers and a trailing habit. Neither of these latter two should be pruned regularly as they flower on old wood. *B. alternifolia* can be grown on a standard stem to make a small weeping tree. There are a number of other buddleias that are either tender or less drought tolerant and so less suited to the waterwise garden.

Callistemon
Myrtaceae
These are the bottlebrush plants from Australia. Once established they are tolerant of dry soils and all like warm sunny sheltered locations.

One of the best is *C. citrinus*, (Z9) so called for its lemon scented foliage. The cultivar 'Splendens' AGM has the typical rich red bottlebrush-shaped flowers. As well as the red ones, there are other colours and the yellow flowered *C. pallidus* is particularly stunning when in full flower.

Caragana

Leguminosae/Papilionaceae

Although there are a number of species, the most familiar of these is *C. arborescens* (Z3), pea tree, which is grown as a large shrub or sometimes on a stem as a small tree. It is a thorny plant bearing finely divided pinnate leaves and small yellow pea-like flowers. It is tough, drought and wind resistant and requires minimal maintenance.

C. arborescens 'Pendula' is a trailing form, usually grafted on to a standard stem to make a small weeping tree. It is another useful alternative for a weeping willow under dry conditions and in a small garden.

BELOW Coming from California, all Ceanothus, like this 'Trewithen Blue', will tolerate hot and dry conditions and flower profusely when conditions are favourable.

Ceanothus

Rhamnaceae

Commonly known as the Californian lilacs, these shrubs are generally blue and come from not only California but also Western North America and Mexico. All are tolerant of dry conditions and hot summers. Indeed they are more likely to die of poor drainage and cold wet conditions. Most flower in early

CULTIVATION TIP
There are also the late summer flowering types such as 'Gloire de Versailles' AGM, which should be hard pruned in late spring. This is a blue flowered cultivar but there is also 'Perle' Rose' which is pink and should be treated similarly.

PROPAGATION TIP

Centaurea gymnocarpa can be rooted from semi-ripe cuttings in the autumn. For reliable rooting use the traditional technique of heeled cuttings. These are small sideshoots torn from the main stems with a sliver of old wood. If you want to make sure there are some suitable sideshoots, take the tip out of a few main shoots in late summer to encourage the sideshoots to grow in good time for propagation.

to mid summer and they are generally all in Zone 9 for hardiness.

There are many different species and cultivars from prostrate types such as the slightly tender *C. gloriosus* at a mere 30 cm (1 ft) up to the near tree proportions of *C. arboreus* 'Trewithen Blue', which can make 6 m (20 ft) This latter cultivar is spectacular and flowers from early spring through early summer and sometimes beyond. Most prefer the shelter of a brick wall to perform to their best, as they are on the borderline of hardiness. The confusingly named *C. thyrsiflorus* repens AGM, forms excellent dense ground cover, smotheredd in masses of blue flowers but often making a vigorous plant between 90 cm to 1.8 m (3–6 ft) in height, hardly creeping as the name implies. There is also a white flowered species called *C. incanus*. Most should have minimal pruning, immediately after flowering just to tidy up any leggy shoots.

Cedrus

Pinaceae

There are actually only four species of cedar generally originating from the Western Himalayas and the Mediterranean. All make huge park scale trees and are slow growing

and long lived. Once established all are very tolerant of hot dry conditions. In practical terms, they should generally be considered as short-term temporary trees in most small gardens, to be felled and replaced before they become a nuisance. Probably *C. atlantica glauca* AGM, the Blue Atlas cedar, is the most likely candidate for a smaller garden. It has a well shaped upright habit and produces vivid glaucous blue foliage, looking good even when young. When fully mature it can reach to 40 m (130 ft) so beware when planting.

Centaurea

Asteraceae

These are various forms of the common knapweed, generally called cornflower when annuals. All thrive in poor, well-drained soils. Most of the perennial flowering types are, in my opinion, poor garden plants with sparse flowering. The foliage types are however well worth growing. *C. gymnocarpa* (Z7) is a subshrub making a glorious soft cushion of intricately cut foliage. It makes a short lived perennial lasting several seasons or alternatively can be planted as a bedding plant and propagated annually from autumn cuttings. Botanists prefer to call it *C. cineraria* (Z7), but this does not distinguish it from the bedding types such as 'Silverdust' and 'Cirrus' both of which are grown from seed annually. All of them make excellent foliage in hot dry climates.

Centranthus

Valerianaceae

The red valerian is a common plant often growing wild in many rocky area, cliffs and

RIGHT The bottlebrushes, such as this *Callistemon rigidus*, are good wall shrubs, thriving against a hot sunny wall and rewarding with copious flowers.

abandoned rock gardens. *C. ruber* (Z4), as it is correctly known, is a much undervalued plant as it flowers freely and for an extended period in early summer despite total neglect. It is tough and hardy and gives its best display when soil conditions are poor. There are various white forms of it, such as 'Snowcloud', and a deep red cultivar called 'Atrococcineus'. It self-seeds readily and can be invasive, so the best treatment is to trim back after flowering but before seeding, which will result in a useful smaller second flowering.

Cercis

Leguminosae/Papilionaceae
These are small trees or large shrubs found naturally on rocky hillsides at the edge of woodlands in North America, parts of Asia and the Mediterranean. All are showy plants with pink or white pea-like flowers. They have the ability to flower whilst young, which is rewarding. Also old trees will produce flowers not only where expected on the smaller shoots but also in fascinating little clusters that appear directly from the mature bark. The most familiar is *C. siliquastrum*, (Z7) AGM, the Judas tree, which makes a small, many-stemmed tree up to 10 m (30 ft) in height. It flowers in late spring just before the leaves appear. There is also a less common white flowered form of it.

The purple-leaved form of the Eastern Redbud, *C. canadensis* 'Forest Pansy' (Z4)

BELOW Although slow growing, *Cercis siliquastrum* will flower as quite a small plant on both the young shoots and, in time, the old wood.

AGM, is a spectacular plant. It produces wide, flat heart-shaped leaves in a rich deep lush purple. It can be expensive to purchase but is well worth the investment. It will flower but as its main display is from its foliage it may be worth spring pruning to encourage luxuriant foliage. Both are tolerant of hot dry conditions

Chamaerops
Arecaceae/Palmae
The dwarf fan palm comes from rocky areas of the Mediterranean and is barely frost hardy. It is, however, very tolerant of full sun and dry sandy soils. Botanically known as *C. humilis* AGM, it is grown for its typical fan-shaped palm foliage. It is a small bushy palm and well adapted for growth in a domestic garden, either in the soil or in a planter. If in a container, remember to protect its root system from frost over winter.

Cistus
Cistaceae
These colourful plants, commonly known as rock roses or sun roses, really thrive in hot, dry, sunny locations. They originate from dry, rocky areas of the Canary isles, North Africa, Southern Europe and Turkey. All are shrubby perennials, although they can be short-lived. Most are Zone 8 for hardiness.

C. x *corbariensis* AGM, is one of the best and most reliable whites, producing a mass of white flowers over a compact bush no more than 90 cm (3 ft) in height. *C. populifolius* produces slightly larger and lusher white flowers but is inclined to be tender. The cultivar 'Silver Pink' has soft pink flowers and *C. pulverulentus* 'Sunset' has deep rose pink flowers. All are easy, tolerant shrubs that respond fast and tolerate dry conditions.

Convolvulus
Convolvulaceae
This genus is probably best known for the pestilential and difficult to eradicate weed bindweed. However there are some better behaved and more attractive relations that will fit well in a waterwise garden. *C. sabatius* AGM syn *C. mauritanicus* (Z8) is a small trailing plant that produces a succession of brilliant mid-blue flowers throughout the summer. It makes a good container or basket plant with minimal water requirements. It is best treated as a half hardy perennial. The shrubby *C. cnoerum* (Z8) is grown mainly for its delicate silver foliage, although it does produce sparkling white and yellow centred trumpets in early summer. Given a warm sheltered spot and good drainage it should survive most temperate winters.

Cordyline
Agavaceae
Although known as the cabbage palms, the two species are not related. However given time they will form tall trees with shaggy heads, not unlike palms in overall appearance. They come from open areas, hillsides and scrubland in SE Asia, the Pacific and Australasia. Initially they have one stem with a single tuft of narrow foliage at the top. Over time they may branch and make multi-stemmed specimens. Older plants will flower with a large inflorescence of very sickly sweet smelling white flowers. Nice as a distant drift of perfume but overpowering at close-quarters.

As young plants they are inclined to be tender and need some winter protection. Traditionally the foliage is bunched up and tied to protect the growing points. Older plants tend to be more frost tolerant. They also make excellent container plants, although these are more likely to succumb to frost. All make dominant specimen plants with a strong structural outline, worthy of a prime place in any landscape.

The hardiest of all is *C. australis* (Z9) AGM with plain green foliage. It is tough and relatively fast growing. There are many coloured leaved forms such as *C.* 'Albertii' AGM with variegated foliage, 'Purple Tower' with rich purple foliage, and 'Sundance' with a red midrib. In general the coloured leaved forms are less hardy than the plain green species.

Cortaderia
Graminae/Poaceae
The well known pampas grass has been much maligned in recent years and dismissed as unfashionable, but there are few other grasses that make quite such a bold statement as these. They originate from areas of New Zealand, New Guinea and South America. Once established they need little attention and will tolerate hot dry conditions making spectacular leafy specimens topped with huge white or pale pink plumes in late autumn. A roadside embankment near where I live is dotted with these, which in the autumn each year make a spectacular show and defy the total lack of attention and heavy competition they get from surrounding grasses.

The species *C. selloanna* (Z5) will make 3 m (10 ft) in a season whereas the cultivar 'Pumila' AGM is a veritable dwarf at 1.5 m (5 ft). There are gold and silver variegated types, 'Gold band' and 'Silver Stripe' respectively (both Z8). Both are compact and good foliage plants, although perhaps not as tough and tolerant as the species. *C.* 'Rendatleri' has purplish pink plumes that are somewhat

slender and delicate. The species *C. richardii* (Z8), which grows to 2.5 m (9 ft), is even more delicate in appearance but nevertheless has a certain elegant charm and is very tough and tolerant of neglect and poor conditions.

Cotoneaster
Rosaceae
Another genera of good, tough 'workhorse' plants, generally for use as backgrounds, screens, fillers or tough groundcover. Think of them as the chorus rather than the stars of the show. Nevertheless they do have some attributes. There are many types from dwarf spreading groundcovers through to boisterous types for screening. Most have insignificant white flowers but colourful autumn berries often in profusion. Most are evergreen. All will tolerate reasonable drought once established and are particularly good in dry shade. Their only weakness is the possible infection from fireblight, which can be devastating. The following is just a few out of the vast numbers that are available in the nursery trade.

C. 'Coral Beauty' is a good groundcover growing to a maximum of 90 cm (3 ft) with copious orange fruits. For a good hedge, choose *C. lacteus* AGM which is quite upright and responds well to trimming. It is semi-evergreen and has red berries. *C. salicifolius* makes a tall evergreen bush with arching branches laden with red fruit in the autumn. Another tall one is *C.* 'Rothschildianus' but this time with yellow fruit, quite the exception. *C. horizontalis*, AGM, known as the fishbone cotoneaster, has a compact habit and grows well as a low wall shrub spreading itself tightly against brickwork.

RIGHT *Cordyline australis* makes an excellent centerpiece for this low maintenance planter surrounded by succulent *Aeoniums*.

Although deciduous it has brilliant autumn
colour and a heavy crop of red berries, intricately spaced along the fish-bone stems. There
is a variegated type that is slightly less
vigorous. Finally C.'Hybridus Pendulus' is a
dwarf groundcover type but is often grown
grafted on a tall stem to make a small weeping
standard tree – maybe a bit twee!

Crambe

Brassicaceae/Cruciferae
Best known for the somewhat massive herbaceous perennial *C. cordifolia* AGM (Z5). This
monster makes a huge plant up to 1.8 m
(6 ft) covered in clouds of tiny white flowers
in early summer. The flowers give an effect
like *Gypsophila* but the foliage is broad and
dark green, almost like a rhubarb leaf. It does
not transplant well but has deep tap roots,
which enable it to survive drought, and can
be used for root cuttings. Use it as a statement amongst lower planting. It's relative
C. maritima, (Z5) sea kale, can be eaten as
a vegetable and is also quite attractive with
large blue-grey leaves. It is very tough and
tolerant of many various conditions,
including salt spray.

Cupressus

Cupressacea
This is a group of evegreen conifers, of which
a few are valuable plants for our waterwise
garden. All make upright columnar trees
which, once established, are very drought
tolerant. *C. arizonica var glabra*, despite its
tortuous name, is an attractive plant from
when it is young through to maturity. It has
blue-grey foliage and reddish bark. When
young it forms a tight pyramid but with age it
opens up and becomes somewhat more airy
and delicate. Once it starts to fruit the heavily
laden branches may sag, giving the plants a
more ragged appearance. Those familair with
Italian gardens will know *C. sempervirens* (Z9),
the Italian cypress, familiar for its pencil thin
outline. It is somewhat tender so not suitable
for colder climates.

Cytisus

Leguminosae/Papilionaceae
These are the brooms originating from mountains and scrublands in North Africa, western
Asia and parts of Europe. Most of the brooms
have leaves that are modified to tiny structures
which enable them to survive in very dry conditions. The thin wiry stems are often green and
carry out photosynthesis, which enables them
to compensate for the loss of leaves. They like
hot dry but sheltered sites and will not tolerate
hard pruning.

The common broom that is native to
Europe is *C. scoparius* (Z6), a straggly plant
with yellow flowers. There are then many
hybrids such as 'Hollandia' AGM, cream and
pink, 'Warminster' AGM, creamy yellow and

RIGHT There are several perennial wallflowers such as
Erysimum 'Bowle's Mauve' that perform well with abundant
flowers in the driest of conditions.

'Windlesham Ruby' (not surprisingly red). *C x praecox* (Z7) is a another popular hybrid with pale yellow flowers. All grow to about 1.5 m (5 ft). *C. x beanii* (Z7) is a compact spreading yellow cultivar making a floppy cushion around 60 cm (2 ft) in height but more in its spread.

C. battandierii AGM (Z8) is the odd one out with much larger, three segmented, silvery grey leaves. It flowers with large chunky racemes of bright yellow flowers that smell like old-fashioned pineapple cubes. It grows to as much as 5 m (15 ft), although it can be trained in as a wall shrub on a warm sunny wall. Alternatively it can be grown as a small standard tree.

Dasylirion

Dracaenaceae/Liliaceae

A genus of spiky evergreens from southern USA and Mexico. Makes a complete 'porcupine-like' globe of narrow spiky foliage. Tender, but some gardeners is cooler climates have had success with it in dry sheltered locations. It's very tolerant of drought and gives a fabulous desert atmosphere to the garden.

Dictamnus

Rutaceae

There is only one member of this genus which is found naturally in rocky sites and dry grassland in parts of Europe, Southern and Central Asia through to China and Korea. *D. albus* (Z3) is a herbaceous plant producing spikes of white starry-looking flowers, growing up to about 90 cm (3 ft) There is also a pink form of it known as *D. albus var purpureus*. It's good for mixed plantings with grasses. Both produce an aromatic oil which vaporizes in hot weather and can be ignited without damaging the plant. This is a neat party trick but beware of doing this in drought conditions.

Echinacea

Asteraceae/Compositae

These are the coneflowers, a group of large tall daisies with a prominent central boss, which sticks out like an inverted cone. They come from dry prairies and stony hillsides in areas of North America. They fit in superbly well with mixed prairie plantings and are at their best in late summer.

The species *E. purpurea* (Z3) has pinkish purple petals with a rusty coloured central cone. There are several whites such as *E. purpurea* 'White Swan'. This plant has also been the subject of plant hybridisers recently and several lovely apricot and orange hybrids have been produced. Although the older types are reliable and will tolerate dry conditions, these newer cultivars will need to be tried to establish their toughness and drought tolerance.

Elymus

Poaceae

A genus of blue grasses originating from meadows, prairies and sand dunes in parts of Asia. Sometimes called wheat grass or wild rye, they have tall delicate flower and seed heads. Very striking and tolerant of dry conditions. *E. magellanicus* (Z6) blue wheat grass thrives in a gravel garden. The very invasive plant formerly known as *E. arenarius* has been moved to the genus Leymus

Eryngium

Apiaceae

Those that do not know this genus may neverthless be familiar with the native sea holly, with its prickly bluish grey foliage and blue flowers in midsummer. Struggling as it does on shingly beaches, you will not be surprised that these plants are very drought tolerant. They come from many areas of the world including Europe.

There are several good garden types such as *E.* x *oliverianum* AGM (Z5) which grows to about 90 cm (3 ft) with vivid blue flowers that have a bold central boss to the flower surrounded by prickly spidery bracts of a silvery blue. *A. agavifolium* (Z9) produces a spiky green rosette of foliage, not unlike agave, hence the name. The flower spike is greenish and almost colourless but have a statuesque shape, not dissimilar to teasels from a distance, which can be quite striking.

BELOW An *Eryngium* flowering in late summer, alongside a carpet of pink *Sedum*, providing perfect partners in a hot dry gravel bed.

Erysimum *syn Cheiranthus*
Brassicaceae/Cruciferae

The wallflowers, as they are commonly known, are familiar cottage garden and traditional bedding plants, particularly loved for their

FACT OR FICTION?
Eryyngium giganteum is a biennial, which means it grows one year, flowers the next and then dies after flowering, but usually seeds prolifically. It is sometimes called Miss Willmott's ghost after the 19th century influential gardener Ellen Wilmott. It is said that whenever she visited someone else's garden she would surreptitiously scatter a few seeds of this plant, which would of course come up some time later as a 'haunting' reminder of her visit.

sweet perfume. Most are biennials or short-lived perennials that originate from areas of Europe, Africa, Central Asia and North America. They are so tolerant of dry conditions that they can be found in very dry, inhospitable locations such as growing out of crumbling stone and brickwork – hence the name. They also prefer alkaline soils.

All the biennial seed raised bedding wall-flowers are cultivars of *E. cheirii* (Z7). They will last for more than one year but tend to get leggy and straggly so are best thrown away after flowering. They are easily raised from seed sown outside in early summer each year. 'Blood Red, 'Orange Bedder', and 'Ivory White' are a few of the many cultivars available.

The perennial types are sub-shrubs but they only last for a few years and then growth tends to become weak and straggly. They are easily propagated by cuttings in the autumn so can readily be replaced. One of the best is 'Bowles Mauve' AGM, a soft lavender colour, which flowers for along period in spring and early summer. *E.* x *kewense* 'Harpur Crewe' AGM (Z7) is a lovely old double yellow type with shapely pointed spikes of yellow flowers. Both grow to about 60 cm (2 ft). The perennial types can be lightly trimmed after flower to keep them shapely and vigorous.

Eschscholtzia

Papaveraceae

The California poppy is an extremely colourful, short-lived annual that will provide a splash of vivid colour in even the driest conditions. Originating from dry grasslands in North America it will tolerate quite spartan conditions. Allow it to self-seed amongst ornamental grasses and just weed out the seedlings where they are not wanted. There are various seed mixes but they are generally cultivars of *E. California* AGM. Sow outdoors in situ in mid-spring.

Eucalyptus

Myrtaceae

The gums are a large genus of fast growing evergreen trees found mainly in Australia but also in the Philippines, Malaysia and Indonesia. Their foliage is often greyish and aromatic and the bark, which is white, brown or reddish, often peels in an attractive manner. All are evergreens and very tolerant of drought. Many are very vigorous and will make dominant trees in a landscape crowding out other plants, so choose and locate with care.

Most eucalypts are easily grown from seed. They must be planted as small plants as they resent root disturbance. However they are only small plants for a short time, due to their rapid speed of growth. They are very tolerant of pruning so can be hard pruned each year to ground level or to a short framework and in this way you can keep them as bushes. As such they are unlikely to flower but you will still get lush foliage.

Most eucalypts have two types of foliage. As young plants, or if they have been cut back, they produce leaves in pairs and this is called juvenile foliage. When tree gets older this changes and the tree produces adult foliage, which is often different in shape and the leaves are alternate on the stem.

One if the commonest is *E. gunnii* (Z9) AGM (the cider gum). Young leaves are rounded but older leaves are long and sickle-shaped. The whitish bark is shed annually in late summer to reveal a new layer that is often tinged pink or orange. It is very tough and hardy and will eventually grow into a tree up to

25 m (80 ft) in height. *E. globulus* (Z9) AGM is often seen as small plants used for summer bedding but it can grow up to 2-3 m (6-10 ft) in a season and will make a large tree. *E. perriniana* (Z9) is charming as a young plant as each pair of leaves is fused to appear like a single leaf through which the stem grows. Adult foliage is lance-shaped. For striking bark, choose *E. pauciflora* subsp *niphophila* (Z8), the snow gum, with lovely peeling bark that shows strips of white, brown and grey as it sheds its old 'skin'. A few have showy flowers such as *E. ficifolia* (Z9), which has colourful red blossoms, although the leaves of this are green. This one is less hardy and unlikely to flower cooler climates.

BELOW Sometimes chance seedlings can provide striking combinations like these self-set *Eschscholtzias* and pot marigolds amongst red petunias.

Euonymus
Celastraceae

The spindle bushes are common to the point that in many European landscapes they are often over-used. They are very tough and tolerant of poor conditions and are particularly useful in dry shade. They are another group of good workhorse fillers, rarely centre stage but very useful and reliable. The are usually Zone 5 plants.

Most of the common ones are cultivars of *E. fortunei* and make low mounds of weed resisting, evergreen foliage. 'Silver Queen' AGM is an older cultivar, with prettily variegated white and green foliage, and makes a tidy low cushion. 'Emerald Gaiety' is similar but with pink tints in the winter, although the habit of growth can sometimes be a bit ragged. 'Emerald Gold' is green with golden yellow

margins. 'Blondy' and 'Sunspot' are other similar golden variegated types.

Euonymus europaeus AGM is native to the UK and is also deciduous. 'Red Cascade' is a good cultivar of it, which has excellent dramatic red autumn colour before dropping its foliage. Its fruits are also quite flamboyant, being a rich red with orange centres. Occasionally evergreen types such as 'Silver Queen' can produce similar fruits and the combination of red and orange over the variegated foliage can be quite striking.

Euphorbia

Euphorbiaceae

The spurges are a group of plants that are amazingly wide-varying, and many, but not all, that will tolerate dry conditions. They vary between tough, hardy species through to those like *E. pulcherrima*, the well known Christmas poinsettia, that are quite tender. Most have yellowy green flowers. All have a milky white sap, which is an irritant so great care must be taken when working with them. Some are herbaceous and die down each year, some are shrubs with a permanent framework and many are sub-shrubs which means that their stems last for a couple of years while they grow and then flower and then die to be replaced by more shoots from the base.

One of the most useful for the dry garden is *E. characias* (Z7) which comes in quite a few variations. It makes a striking globe of a plant with many stems crowded with narrow silvery leaves. In early summer each stem is topped with a huge head of limey coloured flowers. There is a subsp called *wulfenii* and a number of named cultivars such as 'Lambrook Gold' and 'Margery Fish'. 'Emmer Green' is an attractively variegated form.

E. mysinites AGM (Z8) is a valuable little groundcover plant that looks best sprawling over the edge of a wall or between rocks. The grey foliage and thick stems are quite succulent, giving a clue as to its drought tolerance. It produces yellow-green flowers in spring, after which the flowered stems should be cut out to allow new shoots to develop. Amazingly it is regarded as a noxious weed in some areas of North America.

One rather choice spurge is *E. mellifera* (Z8). It is an evergreen sub-shrub, and although it only has plain green leaves with a white central vein is still a quite striking plant. Its late spring flowers are a pale biscuity brown and sweetly honey scented. Coming from the Canary Isles and Madeira, it was regarded for many years as too tender for cooler climates, but with global warming it is proving viable in many locations. There are also many succulent tender types that are very drought tolerant but also tender so really beyond the scope of this book.

Euryops

Asteraceae/Compositae

This is a group of small half hardy shrubs with daisy flowers, mainly from Southern Africa. Traditionally they were grown in summer but increasingly we are finding that they will overwinter in sheltered spots with good drainage.

E. chrysanthemoides (Z9) has yellow flowers over a tight cushion of green delicately cut foliage. Flowers are produced in flushes, which means it can be very colourful at times during the summer but then go out of flower for a few weeks before repeating the performance. Its relative *E. pectinatus* (Z9) has slightly

RIGHT The genus *Euonymus* includes many tough groundcover plants such as this gleaming little evergreen cultivar called 'Blondy'.

less flowers but the added benefit of finely cut grey foliage.

Fascicularia

Bromeliaceae

This is a genus of bromeliads. Although many bromeliads are epiphytic and live in trees in tropical areas, *F. bicolour* (Z9) lives in the ground (terrestrial), comes from Chile and is almost hardy. It forms a rosette of dark green spiny narrow foliage. When established, it will produce small pale blue flowers in the crown. Although these in themselves are insignificant, at the same time as flowering the surrounding foliage turns a brilliant scarlet.

Festuca

Poaceae

The fescues include a number of colourful and dainty grasses that thrive in the driest of locations. Many fescues are valuable constituents of lawn grass mixtures, but here we will talk about the ornamentals. Most make little tufty evergreen plants about 20 cm (8 in) tall extending to 45 cm (18 in) at the most when they are flowering.

Most of the useful ones are cultivars of *F. glauca* (Z4). The species has very narrow, thread-like silvery grey foliage and creamy flowers and can be grown from seed. It is as tough as the proverbial 'old boots' and I have seen it thriving on the edge of a roundabout with all the problems of traffic pollution, salt in winter and very little water. Improved forms like 'Elijah's Blue' or 'Blue Fox' have icy blue foliage. 'Golden Toupee' has yellow foliage, which seems to have an underlying hint of the silvery blue of its parent. The fancy coloured leaved forms can be easily divided in the spring.

Foeniculum

Apiaceae

This is more commonly known as the culinary herb fennel, which grows wild in parts of Europe. The species *F. vulgare* (Z5) grows to about 1.5 m (5 ft) with filigree apple green foliage. The leaves have a strong aniseed scent. It is the sort of plant to grow between other bolder foliage, such as *Bergenia*. It is a short-lived perennial but seeds freely and occasional seedlings can often make perfect combinations with other plants. If it appears in the wrong place, quite simply pull it up. Alternatively if you don't want it to seed too freely, remove some or all of the seed heads before they shed. There is a purple leaved form call *F. vulgare* 'Purpureum', which produces a lovely dusky smoky effect. It too will re-generate from its own seed.

Fremontedendron

Sterculiaceae

These wonderful plants originate from mountainous areas of North America and Mexico. They thrive in hot dry areas and are often grown in temperate regions as wall shrubs on a south or west facing wall. They are evergreen shrubs bearing masses of flashy bright yellow, saucer-shaped flowers in early summer. All have hairy shoots and foliage, which can be an irritant, so handle with gloves to avoid problems. The species is *F. californicum* (Z9), although the cultivar 'Californian Glory' AGM is more commonly grown. Other cultivars are available but there seems little difference.

Fremontedendron is one of my all time favourites and I have admired it for years, although it obviously doesn't like me. I have tried to grow it in every garden I have owned and have bought plants numerous times and always failed. However on one occasion I had purchased a plant for one of the estates where I used to work and by mistake it was planted on a cold north facing wall. To my astonishment it grew, thrived and eventually had to be hard pruned when it started to interfere with the gutters. I'm sure it did it to spite me.

Gaillardia
Asteraceae

It is very tempting as an author to leave out plants that you don't like. Well this is one, but I must include as it is colourful and easy to grow. These large colourful daisies are natives of the American prairies and therefore tolerant of hot, dry conditions. They are perennial but often short-lived and can be straggly. The flowers are however vivid with a brownish red centre and radiating petals often in red and yellow. There are a number of cultivars such as 'Dazzler' AGM and 'Kobold' better known by its synonym 'Goblin' (Z4). Having described it I really can't say why I don't like it!

Gazania
Asteraceae/Compositae

These dazzling daisies originate from the meadows of tropical Africa so are unsurprisingly tender. They may have green or silvery grey foliage and this can be attractively lobed. The flowers often exhibit dramatic colour

BELOW The low growing *Genista* 'Lydia' tumbling over the edge of brick steps against *Stachys* 'Primrose Heron' backed by *Rosa* 'Buff Beauty'.

contrast with rings of orange, black, green pink and yellow in amazing combinations. They are most commonly known and used as bedding plants and can be grown from seed or from overwintered cuttings.

The cultivar 'Aztec' has finely-fingered silver foliage with creamy flowers graduating to wine-red. The colouring with Gazania flowers is on each petal so the overall effect is of concentric circles. 'Christopher' has green leaves with flowers that are rich pink with a sage-green zone and yellow centres. The species and older types tend to close their flowers overnight and do not open on dull days, which can be disappointing. Some of the modern cultivars such as the 'Kiss Series' have bred out this characteristic and are more reliable for flowering in dull conditions. These are good bedding plants for containers, where water is in short supply. All are tender (Z9) and must be raised from seed or cuttings overwintered under frost-free glass.

Genista

Leguminosae/Papilionaceae

This is another group of plants sometimes also called broom and are in fact very similar to *Cytisus*, which is a related genus. They come from rocky areas, cliffs and dry pastures in the Mediterranean, Europe and Western Asia. They are all shrubby and characteristically all have yellow pea-like flowers. Like many plants adapted for dry conditions, the leaves are very small but the green stems give them an evergreen appearance

G. hispanica (Z8), Spanish gorse, makes a tight round bun of a plant, which is very prickly and covered in golden yellow blossoms in early summer. Somewhat looser in growth, *G. lydia* (Z8) AGM is best grown over the edge of a low

wall or among rocks where it can naturally tumble and spread. It has masses of yellow flowers in early summer. Contrastingly, *G. aetnensis* (Z8) AGM, the Mount Etna broom, makes a huge shrub or small tree and can grow up to 8 m (25 ft). Its habit of growth is very delicate with slender branches and a weeping open tracery of twigs, which produce a whole cascade of lemon yellow flowers in mid to late summer. It looks best grown with plenty of space around it so that its elegant shape can develop without intrusion or the need to prune.

Gleditschia

Caesalpiniaceae/Leguminosae

Here we have a small group of trees with delicate pinnate foliage, which is the main reason for their choosing them. Sometimes called the honey locusts. Flowers are white and usually insignificant. Most have sharp spines. They are tough, fully hardy and once established are tolerant of hot dry conditions.

The plain species, *G. triacanthos* (Z4) is an elegant tree with glossy green foliage and significant brown seedpods in the autumn. *G.* 'Sunburst' AGM is one of the best golden foliage trees for small gardens, and 'Rubylace' has reddish purple foliage, both making no more than 5 m (15 ft).

Grevillea

Proteaceae

This curious genus originates from Australia, so not surprisingly many are tender. However a few are proving well worth growing in temperate areas with milder winters. All are

RIGHT Both *Fremontedendron californicum* and *Abutilon vitifolium* 'Album' are strong growing wall shrubs that will grow and thrive in hot dry conditions.

evergreen and have fascinating spider-like flowers, often with long slender styles like an insect's proboscis. Be sure to give them warm sheltered spots and good drainage.

G. rosmarinifolia (Z9) AGM is a small bush growing to around 1.2 m (4 ft) with dark green needle-like foliage which looks very similar to a rosemary plant. The flowers, however, are rich rosy-red. In a similar colour we have 'Canberra Gem' AGM, which produces flowers throughout the year but has its main flush in late spring. The species, G. sulphurea (Z9) AGM has attractive pale lemon yellow flowers.

Griselinia

Cornaceae/Griseliniaceae

These are a group of glossy-leaved evergreen shrubs from New Zealand, hardy in all but the harshest of winters. They are useful as background and sheltering plants as they will tolerate windy conditions, but equally are showy enough for a key location. Once estab-lished they will survive without showing undue stress in dry conditions.

G. littoralis (Z8) AGM is the commonest and easiest to obtain with pale green leaves. The flowers are fairly insignificant and not it's best feature. In good conditions it is said to eventually reach 8 m (25 ft) but it can be easily trimmed to keep it within an allotted space or to stop it taking over your garden. The variegated version has irregular white and grey margins and streaks. A particularly fine variegated form is called 'Dixon's Cream' and has central yellow blotches in an uneven pattern. Both grow to about 2.1 m (7 ft). There is a very fine form called. G. lucida (Z8) with mid-green leaves that look quite waxy but it is less hardy.

X Halimiocistus

Cistaceae

The X at the beginning of the name means that these are hybrids and in this case are crosses between *Cistus* and *Halimium*. Some of these are found naturally in hot dry areas in France and Portugal, where both parent species can be found growing. Like both parents they are tolerant of drought and all are low growing. Look out for X H. sahuccii AGM, (Z8) with small white saucer-like flowers and 'Merrist Wood' AGM, which has creamy flowers with a pretty red band.

Halimium

Cistaceae

One of the parents of the above hybrid. These are small but showy shrubs with colourful flowers. Both H. atriplicifolium (Z8) and H. lasianthum (Z8) are yellow flowered and will achieve between 1-1.5 m (3-5 ft). Grow at the front of a border in dry well drained soils.

Hebe

Schrophulariaceae

Opinions vary as to how tolerant Hebes are when faced with drought. Certainly many of them would prefer moist humus-rich soils but will nevertheless survive short periods of drought and hot conditions. They originate from rocky sites and cliffs in areas of New Zealand and Australia and are such a valuable group of plants that they cannot be missed from this list.

They are all evergreen shrubs, varying in height from diminutive ground-hugging cush-ions at less than 30 cm (1 ft) up to vigorous thugs at 2.5 m (8 ft). Few are grown mainly for their foliage but most have attractive spikes of tiny flowers in white through pink to almost red, blues and purples. There are hundreds of both species and hybrids and they are popular plants. Here I mention just a few favourites and those known to be drought tolerant.

H. pinguifolia ' Pagei' AGM (Z6), makes a low carpet plant no more than 15 cm (6 in) tall, with tiny grey leaves that effectively cover the ground. It is tough, hardy and in late spring the plants are covered by white flowers. Another with silver foliage is *H. albicans* AGM (Z6), making a taller mound around 30 cm (1 ft) in height. There is a similar cultivar called 'Red Edge', which is like its parent except for a tiny but significant red margin to each leaf.

BELOW All ivies are evergreen but variegated types such as this 'Goldheart' are particularly valuable in the winter and totally drought tolerant.

H. ochracea 'James Stirling' (Z6) is one of the whipcord Hebes. These have adapted foliage, which is small and scale-like and hugs the stem. The overall effect is a small golden wiry plant like a small juniper. It has white flowers when well established but the foliage is the main feature. Having modified foliage, the whipcord types are very drought tolerant

There are many excellent small compact cultivars that give long displays of flowers in summer. 'Wiri Joy' (Z9) is an attractive pink and 'Alex' (Z8) is a prolific lavender with purple tinted stems. *H. franciscana* 'Variegata' AGM (Z9) has white edged foliage and soft lavender flowers. All three make tight hummocks at less than 90 cm (3 ft) high. 'Great Orme' AGM (Z8) is a bit taller at around 1.2 m (4 ft) with

long pink and white spikes of flower. There are numerous other cultivars available.

Hedera

Araliaceae

The ivies are a very well known group of plants that originate from several areas of the world. In the garden they can be used as climbers on brick walls or trees stumps or as groundcover. They climb by means of aerial roots that grow into cracks and crevices so are no good on trellises or smooth structures unless they are tied in place. They will be at their most lush in soils that are moist and rich in humus but once established will tolerate some water shortage.

There are several large leaved types such as *H. colchica dentata* AGM (Z6) which has large leathery green leaves. Then there is *H. canariensis* 'Gloire de Marengo' AGM (Z8), which is similar but variegated with irregular white margins, or 'Sulphur Heart' AGM syn 'Paddy's Pride' (Z6) with green leaves generously splashed with gold. This latter is a fabulous plant with lovely winter colour.

H. helix (Z5) is the common English ivy which has a relatively small leaf. There are hundreds of cultivars of this with gold or silver variegations and many different leaf shapes. The simplest, plainest types are likely to be the toughest in drought conditions. In very hot, dry conditions red spider mite may also be a problem with this plant. A possible for the dry garden but not the ideal choice.

Helianthemum

Cistaceae

These small leaved and colourful plants are more commonly known as rock roses. They grow to no more than around 30 cm (12 in) making little mounds of tiny evergreen foliage.

In early summer they are covered with myriads of small penny-round flowers in all colours except blue. There are many named hybrids but these can also easily be grown from seed, which provides a cheap way of raising a quantity of plants. Generally Zone 7.

Helichryssum

Asteraceae/Compositae

These are a tough bunch of shrubby plants, mostly with silver foliage and largely very drought tolerant. They are mainly grown for their foliage as the flowers with most of them are insignificant or quite unattractive. Some of the commonest are known as curry plants because of the strong aroma of supermarket curry powder. *H. italicum* ssp *serotinum* AGM, (Z9) is one such plant with attractive small leaves like a very white lavender. It grows to about 60 cm (2 ft). *H. splendidum* AGM (Z8) has a slightly more ragged woolly look to it and doesn't have the strong smell. Both of these are tough and hardy.

H. petiolare (Z9) is a familiar basket and patio plant, available each spring as small plants. It forms a soft cushion of prostrate silvery white foliage, which can be inclined to swamp other plants in a small hanging basket – the baby cuckoo effect. It comes into its own as a silvery groundcover plant or for use in a large planter where watering is restricted. It is very tough and drought tolerant. There is a lovely soft sulphurry yellow form of it called 'Limelight', a rather course variegated one and some more compact forms such as 'Goring Silver'.

RIGHT Bearded iris, cultivars of *Iris germanica*, will be at their best where their root-run is hot and dry, resulting in profuse early-summer flowering.

Helictotrichon

Poaceae

A genus of elegant silvery leaved grasses coming from dry hillsides and woodland edges in many parts of the world. The most commonly grown is *H. sempervirens*, AGM (Z4) (oat grass), which used to be called Avena candida until the botanists changed it. It makes a quite striking grass with foliage growing to about 45 cm (18 in) topped with waving pale biscuit brown, oat-like flower and seed heads which take the overall height to around 90 cm (3 ft). It is easy to grow and tolerant of dry conditions but doesn't like wet winters so be sure to give it good drainage. In the spring clean out the dead foliage and old flowers stalks to avoid rot setting in.

Hieracium

Asteraceae/Compositae

A vast family known mainly for its weed species, commonly called hawkweeds. A few are worth growing in the ornamental garden but can seed freely, so monitor carefully and possibly remove the seed heads before they disperse. *H. lanatum* (Z7) is one that is more choice with woolly silver coloured foliage and golden yellow dandelion-like flowers. They grow well in full sun on dry soils so suitable for the gravel garden or other informal areas.

Hippophae

Elaeagnaceae

The commonly grown species is *H. rhamnoides* (Z4) which is a native to Europe. It is found naturally in coastal areas and on rough mountainside screes. It produces a big thicket of vigorous stems, making a bush around 1.8 m (6 ft) tall and wide. It is a good, tough background , screening or shel-terbelt plant. The foliage is small linear and silvery grey. Flowers are insignificant but the female bushes give a rewarding show of bright orange berries that the birds do not seem to like, so the display lasts throughout the winter.

Holcus

Poaceae

Another group of grasses coming from wastelands and woodlands in several parts of the world. They are fairly drought tolerant. The most commonly grown is *H. mollis* 'Albovariegatus' (Z5). This forms a tidy little clump of low growing creamy striped foliage, topped in midsummer with soft, fluffy, grey-green flower spikes. It is easy to grow and increases nicely without being invasive.

Indigofera

Leguminosae

These are shrubs with delicate pinnate foliage and pink or purple flowers. They are easy to grow, very tolerant of dry conditions and have a long flowering season so should be more widely grown. *I. amblyantha* AGM (Z7) looks rather like up upside down wisteria with upright flower spikes in soft lavender. You may also come across *I. hererantha* AGM (Z7) which is more pink and bears slightly less flowers. Both grow to about 1.8 m (6 ft) and can be pruned hard in early spring as they flower late in the summer. Easily confused with *Lespedeza*.

RIGHT This is *Iris unguicularis*, which will thrill us with vivid blue flowers in mid winter, produced on plants growing in a dry spot against the bottom of a sunny wall.

Iris

Iridaceae

This is a vast family of plants with many species and thousands of cultivars. Although many like moist or even waterside conditions there are some that thrive in hot dry baked conditions. All have narrow linear foliage, most are deciduous herbaceous plants or bulbs and a few are evergreen. Many are specialists plants that have been highly hybridised and some become very desirable collectors plants.

One of the best for dry parched conditions is *I. unguicularis* AGM (Z7) which used to be simply called *I. stylosa*. This originates from hot areas of the Mediterranean. Grow it in a really dry location such as at the base of a sun-baked wall. It makes a small compact clump of narrow evergreen foliage which is topped with exquisite blue iris flowers marked with yellow and white. These appear in midwinter and although they may be damaged by hard frost are soon replaced by newly opening buds. It resents disturbance so plant and leave alone. There is a good white form simply called *I. unguicularis* 'Alba' and a cultivar called 'Mary Barnard' AGM with slightly larger violet flowers.

One of the largest groups and probably the most popular are the bearded iris, with their classic *fleur de lis* shape. There are many thousands of hybrids which are popular in many temperate areas. Bearded iris grow from a fleshy rhizome that sits on the surface of the soil. Foliage is a fan of narrow dagger-shaped leaves which die down in the winter. Several flowers are produced at the top of a fleshy stem. Typically there are three petals called the 'falls' which curve down and are topped with a furry 'beard', often in a contrasting colour. In between there are three other petals that are vertical or incurving and are called the 'stan-dards'. As well as the normal border types that grow to about 45-60 cm (18-24 in) there are also some quite diminutive dwarf cultivars. Mostly Zone 5.

They are available in myriads of wonderful and striking colour combinations. When flowering in early summer, they make a spectacular sight. However the display is short-lived and for the rest of the year they are miserable scruffy plants so avoid them in small gardens, where every inch counts. Grow them in larger gardens in an area that can be avoided out of season – or enjoy them in other people's gardens!

Most of the bulbous iris such as the blue *I. reticulata* AGM and its yellow counterpart *I. danfordiae* are quite happy in a dry location as these flower in late winter and then go dormant before the hottest and driest parts of the summer.

I. foetidissima (Z7) is known as the stinking iris because of its pungent foliage. It has evergreen foliage in a deep bottle green. The flowers borne in early summer are a dull, smoky lavender but these are followed in autumn and early winter by seed pods displaying brilliant red, orange or white seeds that come as a welcome surprise on an otherwise shy and retiring plant. Worth using in a dull corner. There is also a variegated form.

These should be divided and replanted in midsummer, every three or four years. Lift the clumps and separate with a knife to individual fans, reducing the rhizome to about 10 cm (4 in). Prepare a well drained, very sunny spot by lightly cultivating. They do not need a rich soil. Reduce the top growth by 50 per cent and replant with the roots in the soil and the rhizome on the surface. Point all the plants in the same direction, usually towards the front of the border for a tidy effect.

Juniperus

Cupressaceae

The junipers are generally a tough group of evergreen conifers that, once established, will tolerate periods of dry and hot weather without undue damage. They are a varied group of plants with some small trees but it is the groundcover plants that are probably of greatest value. There are many species and cultivars and the following is a small selection. Some have sharp needle-like foliage that may cause an irritable rash when they are handled. Generally all are hardy.

Amongst the good groundcover types we have *J. x pfitzeriana* AGM (Z3), which is a vigorous growing plant with mid green foliage making a layered bush up to around 1.2 m (4 ft) but probably double that in width. It's a big plant. The golden form, *J. x pfitzeriana*

BELOW The blue foliage of *Juniperus procumbens* is a cool contrast to the gravel mulch which enables it to grow and thrive through times of reduced water.

ROCKERY CONIFERS

Do beware of cheap collections of so-called rockery conifers. Because virtually all conifers make attractive plants when small, it is all too easy for unscrupulous nurseries to deliberately underestimate the eventual size of some plants and promote them as suitable for rockeries and small gardens. Mentioned elsewhere on this page is 'Skyrocket' that can make a tree of 6 m (20 ft) and *J.* x *pfitzeriana* that can spread to 3 m (9 ft) They can soon become monsters smothering choicer plants. The same can happen with other conifers. When making serious purchases of conifers in particular do check the ultimate sizes before planting.

'Aurea' has golden foliage and is slightly less vigorous. 'Gold Coast' is even more compact and has bright chrome yellow leaves. *J. sabina var. tamariscifolia* (Z3) makes a good flat dark green carpet topping out at no more than 45 cm (18 in). Under nursery conditions, where it will be frequently irrigated it can be very prone to the disease phytophthera, but once established in the garden under drier conditions it is usually trouble free.

The cultivar 'Grey Owl' AGM makes a good flat carpet of soft silvery grey foliage now more than 30 cm (1 ft) in height, but two to three times that in width. It is excellent groundcover. Mention should be made of *J. squamata* 'Blue Star' AGM (Z5) because of its exceptional silvery-blue colour, although I find it an untidy plant with a lumpy habit and too slow to be of great value. Just my opinion though...

Amongst the erect forms we have *J. communis* 'Hibernica' which makes a prickly looking tight column of pale greyish green foliage ultimately reaching 3-5 m (10-15 ft).

J. scopularum 'Skyrocket' (Z3) is a more recent cultivar with a narrow vertical habit of growth, which has the unfortunate habit of spreading with age. However its worth growing for its early years. It should never be considered as permanent – some need to be enjoyed for a few years and thrown away. For one with tree proportions choose *J. recurva*, the Himalayan weeping juniper. In time it will make up to 10 m (30 ft) with a nice rounded cone shape and bright green foliage that weeps at the tips. The bark is orange brown and peels attractively.

Kniphofia
Asphodelaceae/Liliaceae

This familiar group of 'old fashioned' garden plants are commonly known as red hot pokers. This name is really no longer a good description as these plants are now available in a tantalising range not only of reds but shades of orange, yellow and cool limey green. Hardly red hot. The species mostly come from rough grasslands in Africa but many have been hybridised in recent years. Although they prefer a moist humus rich soil, once established they are very tolerant of hot dry conditions. Some are evergreen and some deciduous, all with narrow linear foliage. All produce tall spikes of small tubular flowers.

PLANTING TIP

Use kniphofias towards the back of the border as their foliage is not always tidy. Plant a soft silver plant such as *Centaurea gymnocarpa* in front to hide the base and something tall with purple foliage, maybe a *Berberis* x *ottawensis* 'Superba' behind, to act as a foil.

The actual flower spike will vary from being very narrow, for example with 'Little Maid', to others such as *K. rooperi* (Z6) which are almost rounded.

The cultivar 'Royal Standard' AGM (Z6) is a typical traditional 'poker' with a two tone flower head. The buds at the top of the spike are deep red opening to orange and yellow down the spike. Its grows to around 90 cm (3 ft). If you want an all red one try 'Prince Igor' (Z6), although it's a tall one at 1.8 m (6 ft). 'Percy's Pride must be mentioned as it's a limey green colour and the spike tapers neatly in both directions. For a soft orange, plant 'Bees' Sunset' (Z6). Finally 'Little Maid' AGM (Z6) must be included as it's a delicate lemon-ivory colour and grows to only 45 cm (18 in) with narrow, almost grass-like foliage.

Koeleria

Poaceae

A group of grasses from dry grasslands and rocky areas. The most interesting is *K. glauca*, (Z4) blue hair grass which looks like a slightly bolder, coarser version of *Festuca glauca*. It is evergreen and grows to about 40 cm (16 in) with cream-coloured flower heads.

Koelreuteria

Sapindaceae

Small group of compact trees from dry woodlands in China, Taiwan and Korea. Mainly known for the species *K. paniculata* AGM (Z5), the golden rain tree, which should be more widely grown. The foliage is handsome with

BELOW Stately spires of this red hot poker provide a fitting framework for the chimneys in the background.

pinnate leaves, with each leaflet being finely-toothed. In midsummer the tree produces thin, airy panicles of tiny golden yellow flowers, which en masse are quite spectacular. In the autumn it has a bonus of bladder-like fruits and golden autumn tints before the foliage drops. It can eventually reach 10 m (30 ft) but is relatively slow growing and so suitable for a small garden. It flowers when quite young.

Lamium

Labiatae

The dead nettles are such an easy and tolerant group of plants that they must be included here and indeed they will grow in almost any conditions. However they will not be at their best in dry conditions and they may become prone to mildew. They all make low spreading clumps of groundcover.

Lamium maculatum (Z3) itself would be considered as a weed but there are several cultivars with attractive foliage and flowers. 'Beacon Silver' has silver variegated leaves and pink flowers. 'White Nancy' AGM is similar, but with white flowers and 'Cannon's Gold' has golden foliage and pink flowers. All grow to about 15 cm (6 in) but can spread to make clumps 60 cm (2 ft) or more in width.

Its relative, *L. galeobdolon* (Z4) (yellow archangel), is even more vigorous with long trailing stems. These stems take root when they touch the ground. It is prettily variegated and has yellow flowers but does have a tendancy to become a bit of a menace. It has escaped from gardens many times and can often be found growing in the wild. The cultivar 'Hermann's Pride' is better behaved and less invasive with striking silver variegation, and may make a better choice.

Lavandula

Labiateae/Lamiaceae

The lavenders need little introduction. These wonderful aromatic plants are just as much at home sprawling over rocks in an informal gravel garden as they are lining a formal walkway or in the colourful muddle of a traditional cottage garden. They come from sunny rocky areas of the Mediterranean, the Canary Isles and parts of Africa, Asia and India. Both foliage and flowers are fragrant. There are many tender types as well as the familiar hardy ones.

Most of the hardy types are cultivars of *L. angustifolia* (Z5) which grows to about 90 cm (3 ft) with the typical soft purple flowers and grey foliage. 'Hidcote' AGM and 'Munstead' are both more compact and 'Nana Alba' is a dwarf white.

My favourite hybrid is 'Grosso' which makes a compact bush topped with a profusion of deep blue/purple flower heads on long delicate stems. Then there is *L. stoechas* AGM (Z9) the French lavender has curious dark purple flowers in spring with lighter purple bracts.

RIGHT Lavender is one of those plants that is equally at home in the Mediterranean garden or a classic cottage garden, providing it has good drainage.

Lavatera

Malvaceae

These are the cultivated mallows which originate from many parts of the world including Europe. There are annuals as well as biennials and some short-lived perennials. In particular 'Barnsley' AGM is a very free-flowering shrubby cultivar that makes a vigorous bush covered in pale pink flowers in early summer. To keep it compact it should be pruned hard each spring. Mostly Z9.

Leymus

Poaceae

This is a much maligned but very attractive ornamental grass. The species *L. arenarius* (Z4) has intense steely blue foliage growing to around 60 cm (24 in) topped by long stalks of golden rye-like flowers. Its bad reputation comes from its invasive habit but why blame the plant rather than the gardener who has planted it in the wrong place. Use it where its strong roots can be utilised to stabilise a loose bank of soil or in a really dry inhospitable patch of soil, even in shade. It will grow almost anywhere.

Ligustrum

Oleaceae

Another group of plants known for its poor cousin, the common privet, which is often mindlessly used for dreary hedging. It is admittedly easy and tolerant but makes all the surrounding soil totally impoverished and unsuitable for growing anything else. However this humble subject has a number of far superior relatives that are well worth while growing.

My favourite is *L. lucidum* AGM (Z8), the Chinese privet. This makes a large shrub or ultimately a small tree up to 10 m (30 ft). It has glossy evergreen foliage and in late summer produces tapering panicles of delicate, tiny creamy-white flowers, which are followed by black berries. There is a yellow variegated form called 'Excelsum Superbum' AGM and another called 'Tricolour' which has white variegated leaves with touches of pink. The latter is a bit inclined to be tender.

L. japonicum (Z7) is a similar evergreen but only growing to about 3 m (10 ft). It has a compact form with very tightly set leaves called 'Rotundifolium'. *L. sinense* (Z6) is only a semi-evergreen so slightly less valuable but it has a variegated form. *L. quihoui* AGM (Z6) is also worth trying. All these choice 'privets' make good background or specimen shrubs and once established are very tolerant of dry conditions including partial shade. They should be more widely grown.

Limonium

Plumbaginaceae

These are the statices or sea lavenders which not surprisingly are tolerant of maritime conditions. Although not favourites of mine, they are easy and tolerant of dry conditions. Amongst the perennials we have *L. platyphyllum* syn *L. latifolium* (Z5) which makes a rosette of leathery foliage topped with sprays of feathery violet flowers in late summer. There are also many annual strains of *Limonium* and these are often grown for drying.

Liriope

Convallariaceae

Here we have a small group of evergreen herbaceous perennials that make small tufts of strap-like foliage growing to around 30 cm (12 in). They originate from scrubby areas in China and Japan. These are tough little plants and often seen as groundcover in landscape schemes, although less regularly used in cooler climates.

L. muscari (Z6) is probably the most easily obtained with dark green leathery leaves and spikes of tightly packed small bobbly violet flowers produced in late summer. There are various cultivars, some of dubious value. 'Gold Banded' has a central yellow stripe, 'Silver Ribbon' has silvery foliage and 'Monroe White' has white flowers.

You may also find L. spicata (Z6) with narrow grass-like foliage and pale lavender flowers. It has spreading roots and is good for soil stabilisation. There is also a white flowered form of this, 'Alba' and one with white striped foliage called 'Silver Dragon'.

Lotus

Leguminosae/Papilionaceae

This genus is most commonly known for the feathery filigree trailing plants commonly used in hanging baskets. These are usually either *L. berthelotii* AGM (Z10) with silver foliage and red flowers like lobster claws or *L. maculatus*, (Z10) which is similar with yellow flowers. Both trail to as much as much as 1.8 m (6 ft) in a single season. Flowering only occurs on second year growths so unless you can keep the plants overwinter, consider as foliage plants only. They are both tender but excellent in a basket or container where water may be limited.

BELOW This silver leaved *Lotus berthelotii*, whilst charming on its own, is made into a star attraction using this glazed terracotta pot in gleaming red.

For general garden planting *L. hirsutus*, syn *Dorycnium hirsutum* (Z8) is more suitable. This makes a small elegant shrub up to about 60 cm (2 ft) with dainty silver-grey leaves and creamy pink flowers that at a glance look like clover heads. It comes from Portugal and is of borderline hardiness but worth trying in a dry sheltered spot.

Lupinus
Leguminosae
Lupins are well-known, old fashioned cottage garden plants, mainly recognized for their classic Russell lupins with tall multi-coloured spikes. These are not particularly useful for the dry garden but a few other related species are.

The tree lupin, *L. arboreus* AGM (Z8) from California, is much more suitable. It is a fast growing, somewhat lax shrub, which bears a mass of pale yellow lupin spikes in early summer. It grows to about 1.8 m (6 ft). Use it as a background filler and just once a year it will 'leap out' with an unexpected display. At the other end of the scale the diminutive *L. chamissonis* (Z8) has silvery leaves and tiny lilac blue flowers. A plant for the front of the border or a rock garden. The annual *L. texensis*, (Z3) Texas bluebonnet may be worth trying.

Lychnis
Caryophyllaceae
A genus of rather brashly coloured herbaceous perennials. But personal bias aside, they most are again drought tolerant. The most familiar is *L. coronaria* (Z4) 'Dusty Miller', which is an upright plant with silver foliage and vivid cerise flowers. It reaches to 45 cm (18 in) but can be short-lived. However easy and useful this plant may be, I personally find it rather strident. There is a

white form of it, 'Alba' AGM, that is much more refined. *L. chalcedonica* AGM (Z4), the Maltese Cross, is just as garish with hard red flowers on stiff stems.

Mahonia
Berberidaceae
Now here we have a genus of fabulous evergreen shrubs with scented yellow flowers in winter and spring. Most, it has to be said, would prefer to grow in moist soil and partial shade, but being extremely tolerant they will survive through drought periods.

M. aquifolium (Oregon grape) (Z5) is probably the toughest of all. This is a suckering shrub growing to about 90 cm (3 ft) in height. It makes excellent groundcover in almost any situation, sun and shade, is evergreen and produces chrome yellow flowers in tight clusters in late spring. There are various cultivars that differ a little including 'Atropurpurea', which has purple tinted foliage in winter.

The taller types such as *M. japonica* (Z7) and the hybrids such as 'Charity' and 'Winter Sun' grow to around 1.8 m (6 ft) and flower in midwinter with a delicate perfume. These are the types that prefer moisture and shade but will nevertheless survive some dry conditions when well established.

Nerine
Amaryllidaceae
All of these are bulbous plants, most of which come from stony mountainous areas of Africa. In the garden they thrive in dry sun-baked spots at the base of walls or can be grown in pots. They are dormant in summer during the

RIGHT Although inclined to be invasive, the steely coloured foliage of this *Leymus arenarius* makes it a desirable inclusion for a mixed border.

hottest, driest weather and then throw up 'naked' flower spikes in autumn. The foliage follows the flowers.

The most familiar is *N. bowdenii* AGM (Z8). This produces a slender stem of around 45 cm (18 in) with an umbel bearing widely-spaced bright cerise pink flowers. It likes to be planted and left to establish over a few years and then will give its best display. There is a naturally occurring white form, correctly named *N. f. alba*. There is also *N. sarniensis*, the Guernsey lily, which is similar but with dark salmon pink flowers in closely packed heads.

Nepeta
Labiatae/Lamiaceae
This genus is most commonly known for the familiar catmint, beloved of felines and cottage gardeners. This is *N.* x *faassenii* syn *N. mussinii* (Z4) which makes a low floppy herbaceous plant with grey foliage and lavender blue flowers. The whole plant is strongly aromatic. A more vigorous form of this is known as 'Six Hills Giant'. There is also *N. govaniana* (Z5) which has non-typical pale yellow flowers. All are easy plants to grow, useful for edging a border and tolerant of dry soils.

Nerium
Apocynaceae
Here we have the oleanders that have traditionally been regarded as tropical plants but in recent years they have been tried in more temperate areas and have proved to be tougher than expected. The are highly toxic and should be handled with great care. Never use any of the cut stems for any purpose. All make lax evergreen shrubs up to as much as 6 m (20 ft). In mild areas they can also be trained as standard trees and make superb specimens

as such. They are all cultivars of *N. oleander* (Z9). Flowers come in large clusters in shades of pink, salmon, white and red. There are some with variegated foliage. In temperate areas plant in a sheltered spot, ideally against a wall. They are very drought tolerant. If in doubt of winter hardiness, provide some winter protection with a wrap of fleece packed loosely with straw amongst the branches.

Olea
Oleacea
As a native of Mediterranean areas through to Africa and Australia this is usually grown in far warmer climates. However as the seasons have altered in more temperate areas it has become quite possible to grow this classic tree and already a commercial olive orchard has been planted in the UK, in advance of further warming. Just last year a sizeable crop of fruit ripened on the ancient olive tree that grows in the grounds of the Chelsea Physic Garden in London.

The fruiting olive is *O. europea* AGM (Z9) which is an evergreen tree with leathery greyish leaves. It has tiny white perfumed flowers but it is mainly grown for the edible green fruits which turn black when ripe. Old trees have gnarled shapes and trunks that are full of character. In recent years a trade has developed in old cropped out olive trees that have been headed back, potted and imported. They can be expensive but provide a great feature tree for a Mediterranean style garden.

Olearia
Asteraceae/Compositae
Commonly known as the daisy bushes, many of these come from scrubby and mountainous areas of Australia and New Zealand. They are

naturally tolerant of dry conditions. Most will also withstand salt spray and so may be useful as a windbreak in maritime areas. Some are on the borderline of hardiness so choose carefully. As well as those suitable for screening and backgrounds there are also some smaller and more decorative species that are worth a place centre-stage.

O. *macrodonta* AGM is a tall shrub with glossy, toothed evergreen leaves, growing to about 3 m (10 ft). It is somewhat spoiled when in flower as the profusion of flowers are a slightly dirty white. O. *traversii* comes in a similar category as a tall evergreen with white flowers although the foliage is smaller and less attractive. Both are good background plants.

BELOW Produced in late summer on leafless stems, these shrieking pink *Nerine bowdenii* appear from bulbs that thrive in hot baked conditions.

For the front of the border you could try O. x *scilloniensis* which makes a dense rounded shrub absolutely covered in tiny white starry daisies. In time it can grow into a tall gaunt shrub but is better propagated and replaced as young plants are tidier. The cultivar 'Master Michael' has blue flowers and greyish foliage.

Onopordum
Asteraceae/Compositae

The species most commonly grown is O. *acanthium*, which is a fun biennial and very easy to grow. In appearance it has some characteristics of a thistle but provides a much more dramatic effect. The leaves are huge, spiny toothed and silver in colour. During the first year after sowing the plant just makes an attractive rosette maybe 30 cm (12 in) high. However in the second year it elongates to a stately spire of silver foliage,

topped eventually at over 1.8 m (6 ft) by a few pink-purple thistle heads. At this stage it often gets untidy with leaves dying back, often with mildew. Save just the odd plant to get a few seeds for next year. It is not unduly invasive so it can be allowed to seed within limits.

Opuntia
Cactaceae
This is a typical 'wild west' cactus and very much of a long shot gamble as it's a native of Mexico and really needs to be kept well above freezing. The hardiest is likely to be *O. robusta* (Z8) with the typical spiny flat green pads. If you are lucky, yellow flowers and dark red fruits may be produced. This will need a very well-drained soil with plenty of grit and a sheltered spot, such as under the eaves of the house, where it will remain dry and warm in winter. Having said that there are quite a few people experimenting with cacti outside in temperate areas and achieving some levels of success. Needless to say these will tolerate any amount of drought.

Osteospermum
Asteraceae/Compositae
This is a fabulous genus of exotic daisy flowers in a dazzling range of colours. They come mainly from rocky and scrubby areas in South Africa and are of borderline hardiness. Some are much tougher than others. As well as perennial types there are some annuals that can be grown from seed. All like hot dry locations and will flower best when the soil is poor. I have in the past seen some wonderful displays of these growing in the crevices of dry stone walls in Cornwall in England.

O. jucundum AGM (Z9) is one of the toughest and easiest species. It is a prostrate, compact plant that is covered in bright sugar pink daisies from early summer though to autumn. I once saw it planted amongst grass in a flowering meadow and have to say that, although unusual, it did look striking. There is a compact form of it that is very frost hardy.

Another one that is virtually hardy is *O. ecklonis* (Z9), which produces white flowers with a blue reverse to the petals. It is somewhat more straggly in growth. There are numerous other named cultivars that are likely to be less hardy and these should be propagated by cuttings in the autumn and kept under frost-free glass.

Ozothamnus
Asteraceae/Compositae
Here we have a group of plants, mainly shrubs from New Zealand. Many are small in stature and so need to be at the front of the border or in a container. They like a well drained soil and a sunny sheltered position.

O. rosmarinifolia (Z9) has small white flowers and leaves, not surprisingly like a green rosemary. Its cultivar 'Silver Jubilee' AGM has silvery grey leaves. *O. ledifolius* AGM, the Kerosene bush, is said to have a fragrance like stewed prunes. You might also look out for *O.coralloides* AGM (Z8)which makes a small compact mound with leathery swollen, scale-like leaves .

Papaver
Papaveraceae
Poppies are recognisable to almost everyone, although they do come in a wide range of colours and may be annuals, biennials or

RIGHT Osteospermums thrive on neglect and a hot, dry, sunny position will result in a carpet of glistening summer flowers.

perennials. Most have short-lived, bowl-shaped flowers and in general they all tolerate hot dry soils, although this may shorten the flowering span of annual types.

In dry climates cultivars of the Iceland poppy *P. nudicaule* (Z4) are often used for bedding. These come in yellows, orange and white. *P. rhoeas* is the common cornfield poppy, naturally producing red flowers. There are various mixtures of this, such as the 'Shirley Series', with delicately crinkled red, pink, white and dusky mauve flowers. Also amongst the annuals we have *P. somniferum* AGM (Z8) the opium poppy, which naturally has smoky pink-mauve flowers and grey lustrous foliage. It is also available in other colours and as a double form. It is poisonous but the seed-heads can be dried for winter decoration. I must also mention the somewhat frail *P. commutatum* which has red, typical cornfield poppy flowers but with black blotches, sometimes called the ladybird poppy. All of these are annuals.

The oriental poppy, *P. orientale* (Z7) is a perennial and has many cultivars. They produce bristly stems up between 60-90 cm (2-3 ft) topped with huge floppy bowl-shaped flowers. The blooms are short-lived but spectacular for their fleeting display. There are many reds such as 'Beauty of Livermore' AGM. As well as pure whites, there is 'Black and White' AGM which has white petals with black blotches and striking black stamens. Then we have a few pinks such as 'Cedric Morris' AGM and some mysterious looking smoky purples including 'Patty's Plum'. Although all of these provide a striking patch of colour in early summer, they look untidy after flowering. Position them away from the front of the border and behind something which will grow

up and take over the display for later in the season. It is also worth trimming them down after flowering.

Parahebe
Scrophulariaceae
This small genus comes from dry stony areas of New Zealand and Australia. They make compact evergreen shrubs, are generally hardy and tolerant of dry conditions.

P. catarractae AGM grows to about 30 cm (12 in) with tiny green leaves. In early summer it will be smothered with small lavender blue, speedwell-like flowers. In a slightly paler pinkish white we have *P. lyalii*. Both are good plants if you want something small and well behaved for the front of the border.

Paulownia
Scrophulariaceae
This genus is known mainly for the foxglove tree *P. tomentosa* AGM (Z5) which is a native of eastern Asia. It needs long hot dry summers to ripen the wood enough to flower the next year. It flowers in late spring with masses of showy lilac flowers which can be damaged with late frosts. In the past this was often regarded purely as a foliage tree and grown for its huge round dinner-plate leaves but with our milder springs and lack of late frosts this will often successfully flower in many UK and temperate areas.

Pelargonium
Geraniaceae
These come generally from South Africa and are mainly tender but very valuable for the summer garden and will sometimes overwinter in a sheltered spot and a mild winter. There are vast numbers of named cultivars and also species

THE SUPRISE ELEMENT

A number of plants, particularly annuals but also some perennials, will seed themselves around your garden with abandon. This may on occasions be a nuisance but it can also bring a very relaxed, natural look to an area with drifts of a plant passing through more contrived groupings. This can be particularly effective in prairie plantings and gravel gardens. Annual poppies are one such plant that produces thousands of seeds, although they will not germinate unless they are scratched or cultivated into the soil.

Many grasses will seed freely. Some bulbs will also do this quite successfully, particularly Alliums and Alstroemeria, although it will usually take two or three years before they will reach flowering size. Others that seed in a similar way include:
Foeniculum vulgare 'Purpureum (Bronze leaved fennel)
Verbena bonariensis
Eschscholtzia californica
Onopordun acanthium
Verbascum bombyciferum
Eryngium giganticum

ABOVE *Verbena bonariensis* will seed all on its own, sending up chance seedlings which mingle freely with neighbours such as this lemon yellow Kniphofia.

although these are less commonly available. They are all very tolerant of drought and neglect and particularly useful for a containers.

As well as the flowering types there are also many foliage types and also the scented leaved types such as the peppermint scented *P. tomentosum* or the lemon scented *P. crispum Variegatum* with spires of small round yellow rimmed leaves. The ivy-leaved types, which are trailing are particularly drought tolerant having glossy almost succulent leaves. Generally zone 9.

Pennisetum

Poaceae

The fountain grasses are a group of feathery grasses with fabulous foliage and long-lasting flower spikes. They come from savannah areas of many parts of the world so only some are frost hardy.

Probably the easiest is *P. alopecuroides* (Z5) with green foliage and large seedheads like fat hairy caterpillars in late summer. It grows to around 90 cm (3 ft). There are various cultivars of this. *P. orientale* (Z6) is the oriental fountain grass which is similar but the flower colour is a dusky pink. One of my all time favourites is *P. setaceum* 'Rubrum' (Z9), the purple fountain grass, which grows to about 60 cm (2 ft). The foliage is a rich ruby colour and the flowers are a soft pink. It is widely used in landscaping in hot dry areas. It is not hardy, but well worth while including in a summer planter.

Penstemon

Scrophulariacea

The penstemons are a vast group of plants including many species from very varied parts of both North and Central America. They have been very popular garden plants for many

years and there are numerous named cultivars. Because they come from very varied conditions it is difficult to make generalisations about those that are drought tolerant. However as a rough guide, many of the smaller-flowered, small-leaved species are more likely to be hardy and drought tolerant rather than the big blowsy hybrids which prefer a moister soil. All need good drainage and a sheltered spot if they are to overwinter in a temperate climate.

P. barbatus (Z6) is a small red flowered species and for lavender flowers grow *P. heterophyllus* (Z8) or P. glaber (Z3). *P. hartwegiii* AGM (Z9) is another red which also has a white counterpart 'Albus'. Amongst the larger flowered type, 'Garnet' now correctly known as 'Andenken an Friedrich Hahn' AGM (Z7) is tough and reliable with wine red flowers. 'Evelyn' (Z7) is a good tough pink.

Perovskia

Labiatae/Lamiaceae

One of a group of late-summer flowering shrubs that are all blue flowered. They originate in rocky areas from Central Asia through to the Himalayas and are all hardy and drought tolerant.

The commonest species is *P. atriplicifolia* (Z6), although it is more commonly seen in nurseries as the cultivar 'Blue Spire' AGM. This makes an upright plant with silvery grey stems and leaves that are richly aromatic. The common name is Russian sage which gives the clue to the smell. In late summer it is covered with a profusion of soft blue flowers like a rather open and airy lavender. When planted in a large drift it is always eye-catching.

RIGHT Although tender, *Pennisetum setaceum* 'Rubrum' is a beautiful low water grass for use in a summer planter, contrasting here with *Plectranthus argentatus*.

Phlomis
Labiatae/Lamiaceae

Another group of plants from the sage family originating from parts of Europe, Asia and North Africa. Most are hardy and all tolerate dry conditions and full sun.

The most familiar is *P. fruticosa* AGM (Z8), the Jerusalem sage. It makes a small open bush with stems up to around 90 cm (3 ft) covered with silvery foliage. It is are topped with bright yellow flowers in mid-summer. It becomes straggly with time but responds well to hard pruning and regenerates vigorously. Its relative *P. italica* (Z9) should be more widely grown. It is similar but with narrow grey leaves and soft smoky lavender-pink flowers.

P. russeliana (Z4) is a somewhat coarse herbaceous perennial but useful for providing tough groundcover in a dry situation. The foliage is green with woolly grey undersides and yellow flowers.

Phoenix
Arecaceae/Palmae

These are tropical palms that come from tropical and sub-tropical areas. Amazingly some have been found to be tough and resilient enough to survive outdoors in sheltered temperate locations. Some authorities insist it needs a minimum temperature of 100°c (212°F) whilst others suggest it will tolerate cold down to as low as -70°c (94°F). Whatever the actual figures may be, they are worth trying in a warm open sheltered site.

P. canariensis AGM (Z9), the Canary Island date palm, is regularly available as a small plant. It has dark green very tough leaflets that are sharp. Take care when handling the plant. Planted in a border amongst other plants,

---

INSTANT PALM TREES
Under temperate conditions we will generally see relatively short young plants, which will have a wide spreading habit but not the typical palm stems. To create more of a 'palm tree' effect plant in a tall container such as a 1.8 m (6 ft) section of drainage pipe. Don't attempt to make this look like a palm stem but just enjoy the effect of palm fronds waving overhead. If grown in tubs or planters remember the root system will be more exposed in a container and will need winter protection.

---

there will be some natural shelter which will help with overwintering. *P. dactylifera* (Z9) is the true date palm and has a similar appearance.

For a small container, the miniature date palm, *P. roebelenii* AGM (Z9) can't be bettered. It is generally available with a stem up to 1.5 m (5 ft) and a small head of typical palm fronds. It appears, as the name suggests, as a miniature date palm and makes a wonderful specimen. It will need some winter protection.

Phormium
Agavaceae/Phormiaceae

The New Zealand flaxes are a collection of strongly architectural plants with narrow sword-like foliage. They are technically evergreen herbaceous perennials, so have year-round value. In recent years they have been highly hybridised and we now have a mouth-watering array of different colours available. Although mainly grown for their foliage, when they do flower, this can be quite spectacular. Most are

RIGHT The many forms of *Phormium tenax*, like this green leaved species, all have the same stark architectural fan shape and narrow sword-like leaves.

SPIKIES

A fair few of the plants recommended in this book are 'spikies'. These are plants with narrow foliage which all emanates from a central crown, often near the ground, giving the plant a sort of hedgehog look. This is no botanical definition, just a general observation. There are also other common characteristics in that the foliage is often succulent and waxy which, combined with the narrowness of the leaf, means that they are likely to be drought tolerant. So in general terms many spikies are good waterwise plants.

Spikies will vary, with some like *Phormium* having soft waving leaves that move in the breeze, compared to others such as *Yucca* which have rigid foliage. Either way they still have this sort of 'punk' habit of growth. Many such as *Yucca* and *Agave* will have sharp spikes on the end of each leaf to protect it from foraging animals in the wild. This may be a problem in a family garden with small children.

All spikies are useful statements in a planting scheme. Their strong outlines catch the eye and as such they can often be used as exclamation points in a planting. Position them in key locations at the end of a border or where you want to make a statement. Make groups of different spikies to thread through a scheme giving it a dynamic element. Spikies also make excellent centrepieces for planters or pots located in a key position.

BELOW As well as using spikies as contrasts amongst other types of plants, grouping them all together gives a very punchy border of strong shapes.

generally hardy, given a sheltered spot and good drainage. The coloured leaves types are less hardy than the green-leaved species. Once established they are tolerant of dry conditions. The smaller hybrids make fabulous container specimens, which can then be planted out when they get too big for their pots.

The most familiar one is *P. tenax* (Z8). Although this is the plain green species, it makes an immense statuesque plant with long waving leaves stretching over 1.8 m (6 ft). The flower stems reach up to 3 m (10 ft) or more with small brick red flowers. These are not that eye-catching but the overall framework and skeletal tracery of the stems against the sky is very pleasing. In a good summer seedheads will follow the flowers and these, with the stems, remain strongly architectural through the winter to the next summer. There is a purple leaved form called 'Purpureum' and a variegated form 'Variegatum', both of which make slightly smaller plants but still with good characteristics and a robust constitution. There is another species, *P. cookianum* (Z8), which is also green leaved and somewhat smaller in stature.

From the many hybrids, I will select just a few that are reliable and personal favourites. 'Yellow Wave' AGM, has an arching habit of growth and a rich golden yellow variegation, growing to about 90 cm (3 ft). There are several with pink tints and in particular I like 'Sundowner' AGM, which has an upright habit of growth with leaves that are a soft mix of bronze, olive, red and pink. It associates well with Canna 'Louis Cayeux'. The cultivar 'Dazzler' has vivid red, pink and green stripes giving an overall very rich effect. 'Platt's Black' has to be mentioned as

it is the darkest of all and quite compact, although I have found it to be a weak grower. There are many more. The coloured leaf forms are generally less hardy so consider as zone 9.

Phygelius
Scrophulariaceae
The Cape figworts originate from South Africa. They are regarded as sub-shrubs, which means that they will form a framework of branches, which may survive in mild winters. Alternatively they can be grown as herbaceous perennials and cut to the ground each winter, which encourages new growth from the base each spring. They prefer moist conditions but once established will tolerate dryish soils. Grow against a warm wall where the framework is more likely to overwinter and flowering will start early.

The common species *P. capensis* AGM (Z8) grows to around 90 cm (3 ft) with delicate waving stems of orange flowers. These have a yellow throat which is rarely seen as the flowers hang down. This is definitely one of those plants that is best seen laying on your back. *P. aequalis* (Z8) is the other species with pinkish flowers. There are many hybrids such as 'Yellow Trumpet' AGM, with yellow flowers, 'Winchester Fanfare' with rich red, yellow throated flowers, 'Sensation' a rich cerise and 'Sunshine', which has golden foliage.

Pinus
Pinaceae
The pines are a large group of evergreen conifers that originate from many parts of the world. There are both tender and hardy conifers, some of which will tolerate dry condi-

tions right through to the heat of the desert. The narrow needle-like leaves are ideally adapted to minimising water loss. Most of them are large trees and therefore only suitable for the largest of gardens or parks.

Amongst those that tolerate dry conditions, we have the common Scot's pine, *P. sylvestris* AGM (Z2), the Corsican pine, *P. nigra var. maritime* (Z5), and the beautiful fine-leaved *P. strobus* (Z3), the Weymouth pine. The latter is attractive as a young plant so can be grown in a small garden but remember to rip out before it gets too big! All these pines make good windbreak plants. In warm locations try the spectacular *P. coulteri* (Z8), the bigcone pine, with long needles and huge cones.

Where space is really tight, try *P. mugo* (Z3), the dwarf mountain pine. Although it will eventually reach 3.5 m (11 ft) it is very slow growing and will for many years be a small chunky shrub-shaped pine. This is a great plant for a rock garden or as a specimen almost anywhere in the garden.

Pittosporum
Pittosporaceae

This is a genus of lovely graceful evergreen shrubs mainly from Australia and New Zealand. They prefer a moist well drained soil but once established will tolerate dry soils and high temperatures. Very adaptable plants! They need sheltered conditions and in particular some of the variegated types can be frost tender in cold areas. The main display is the foliage but some have insignificant, sweetly scented flowers, followed by sticky black seeds.

The most familiar is *P. tennuifolium* AGM (Z9), often seen as foliage with cut flowers in a florist shop. It makes a large upright bush or small tree, with small green leaves. The one in

my Midlands garden is currently as tall as my two storey house and looks like an evergreen birch tree! Many coloured leaves forms of this are available. 'Irene Patterson' AGM, is a good silver variegated one and 'Warnham Gold' has yellow foliage. 'Tom Thumb' AGM, is not only dwarf and compact but one of very few plants that has purple foliage and is evergreen too. 'French Lace' is green leaved but the foliage is slightly smaller than the species and gently wavy.

Somewhat less well known is *P. tobira* AGM, (Z9) which makes a small rounded evergreen shrub with cream scented flowers. There is a variegated form. It can be grown in sheltered areas in temperate regions.

Prunus
Rosaceae

Most of the cherry family are unsuitable for hot dry climates and will suffer with extensive water shortage. However, *P. dulcis*, (Z6) the almond is a classic Mediterranean tree that will tolerate drought, give us a display of blossom and produce a valuable crop even under dry conditions. There are a few other species that are good tough background and groundcover plants.

The common laurel, *P. laurocerasus* AGM, makes a huge evergreen bush with large leaves, ultimately up to 8 m (25 ft), although it can be pruned or trimmed as a hedge. It's a real 'toughie' tolerating almost any conditions. There are many shorter groundcover versions of this with smaller foliage, such as 'Otto Luyken' AGM, which sadly can be seen in any supermarket car park and should be left there! 'Cherry Brandy' and 'Low 'n Green' are much more attractive, the latter being particularly good prostrate groundcover. They are however very tough.

The Portugal laurel, *P. lusitanica* is also worth considering for our waterwise garden. It is another tall evergreen but with less coarse, red-stalked, glossy leaves. It also has a variegated form.

Puya
Bromeliaceae

This is another bromeliad and a real challenge, although some have found that it will overwinter in a sheltered situation in temperate locations. Another plant gamble! The most readily available is *P. chilensis* (Z9). It is a spiky plant with vicious hooked thorns, once described as one of the rottweilers of the plant kingdom! If you are lucky enough to get it to flower, it will produce a huge erect stem of greenish flowers.

Pyracantha
Rosaceae

Other books on drought gardening do not list the firethorns but I have seen them growing successfully in the hot dry conditions of California. They can be grown as free-standing bushes or more often as wall shrubs. These are evergreens with small clusters of uninspiring white flowers in early summer. The plants come to life in the autumn with larges bunches of vivid yellow, orange or red berries. 'Soleil d'Or' is a good yellow cultivar with a slightly weeping habit. 'Orange Glow' AGM is one of my favourites and 'Mohave' is a good red.

Quercus
Fagaceae

The oaks are large genus of woody species, originating from many parts of the northern hemisphere. Virtually all are large forest or parkland trees. When well established they will tolerate some drought and certain species are particularly tolerant of high temperatures.

The evergreen or Holm oak, *Q. ilex* AGM (Z8), is a fabulous evergreen tree originating from parts of Europe. It will eventually make 25m (80ft) although can be pruned and trimmed. *Q. agrifolia*, (Z8) the Californian live oak is similar but smaller. For a curiosity, try *Q. suber*, (Z9) the cork oak. It is worth trying now we have somewhat warmer conditions and is slow growing, so will take a while to outgrow its welcome! Don't expect to harvest your own bottle stoppers for many years though.

Rhaphiolepis
Rosaceae

This is a small group of mainly shrubs from parts of Asia where they are natives of scrubby

RIGHT The recent milder winters in the UK have enabled the growth of borderline plants such as *Quercus suber* (the cork oak) with it's the beautiful bark formation.

areas. These are low growing evergreens with fragrant flowers similar to apple blossom in appearance. You may come across *R × dela-courii*, (Z8) which is pink flowered and also *R. umbellata* AGM, (Z8) which is white flowered. Both are tender and need shelter.

Rhus
Anacardiaceae
Most gardeners would recognise the brightly coloured sumach trees in autumn. The most common species is *R. typhina*, (Z4) which makes a large open rounded shrub about 2.1 m (7 ft) high. The stems are hairy like antlers giving it the full common name of stag's horn sumach. The flower heads are velvety and red. The pinnate foliage turns a brilliant orange in autumn. The selected form 'Laciniata' is the best to grow with finely cut foliage. Again they are drought tolerant when established. Don't dig around them as they sucker prolifically.

BELOW *Rhus typhina* 'Laciniata', the Stag's Horn Sumach, produces its star turn in the autumn when the leaves are a fiery red before falling for the winter.

Robinia

Leguminosae

The locusts or false acacias are graceful trees with delicate, finely cut foliage. Many are thorny and they have the disadvantage of brittle wood so can have the disconcerting habit of dropping branches in later life. For this reason do not plant near to buildings or footpaths.

The most familiar is *R. pseudoacacia* AGM, (Z4) a fast growing, suckering tree with white, slightly perfumed pea-like flowers in early summer. It can grow to as much as 25 m (80 ft) The cultivar 'Frisia' AGM, is a golden leaved form of it which, although very much overplanted, is a superb sunny looking tree and somewhat smaller. For a tight compact head of foliage, grow 'Inermis' syn 'Umbraculifera', very much a 'toy town' tree! All of these have white flowers. There are pink flowered versions such as 'Casque Rouge' and 'Idaho' both of which are lovely.

Romneya

Papaveraceae

This is a small group of suckering sub-shrubs coming from scrubby areas of California and northern Mexico. The foliage is grey and somewhat glaucous. The common species is *R. coulteri* AGM (Z8), the Californian tree poppy. The flowers, which are produced in midsummer, are huge open white poppy flowers with prominent golden stamens. It grows to about 1.2 m (4 ft). This plant dislikes transplanting and can be tricky to establish but once settled in, it can spread vigorously. There are stories of it invading houses and appearing through brickwork and concrete. Grow in a warm sheltered position for the best results.

Rosmarinus

Labiatae/Lamiaceae

The rosemaries come from rocky and scrubby sites in the Mediterranean. They are mainly grown for their evergreen aromatic foliage but they do also flower, usually with small pale blue blossoms in late spring. Foliage is generally narrow and small, greyish green on top and white underneath. The common species is *R. officinalis*, (Z8) a shrub that is very tolerant of hot dry conditions and grows to around 1.5 m (5 ft)

There are many cultivars such as 'Miss Jessopp's Upright' AGM, which is distinctly vertical, 'Severn Sea' AGM, which has particularly bright blue flowers and 'Prostratus' AGM, which makes a plant that is totally flat or trails where it can creep over the edge of something. Looks good over steps as it follows the contours closely. All are very tolerant of dry conditions. The only drawback is that they tend to be relatively short-lived so should propagated and replanted every five or so years.

Rubus

Rosaceae

This large genus includes such things as the edible blackberries and raspberries, which are not particularly tolerant of dry conditions. There are also a number of very tough ground-cover species that can be useful in our water-wise garden.

Probably the most useful is *R. calycinoides* syn *R, pentalobus* (Z7). This makes a low spreading bush no more than 10 cm (4 in) high but spreading indefinitely. Foliage is dark green and evergreen. There are tiny white flowers, which may be followed by red fruits but it is for its dense, ground covering foliage that it is mainly grown. It is valuable on a bank as it roots as it goes and will stabilise loose sandy soils. Somewhat more vigorous and really in the thug category, we have *R. tricolor* (Z7), really just a heavyweight version of *R. calycinoides*. Both of these are very tolerant of heat and drought.

There is also *R. cockburnianus* AGM, (Z6) which makes a huge arching bush over 2 m (6 ft) in height. It comes into its own in winter, when the foliage has dropped revealing branches covered in a chalky white deposit. It is viciously thorny! *R. thibetanus* AGM, sometimes sold as 'Silver Fern, is a more compact plant with a similar effect and slightly smaller thorns. Both are drought tolerant.

Ruta

Rutaceae

These aromatic shrubs come from dry rocky areas of the Mediterranean, the Canary Isles, north Africa and parts of Asia. The most familiar is rue, *R. gravaeolens* (Z5), which although it is often sold alongside herbs, is poisonous and can cause skin irritation!

The cultivar 'Jackman's Blue' AGM, is an improvement on the plain species, making a small bush with delicate blue-grey, finely cut foliage. A few small, dull yellow flowers are formed in summer. Grow in a hot dry sunny spot where its pungent foliage will become apparent. Trim in spring if it becomes straggly.

Salvia

Labiatae/Lamiaceae

Most people know this family for the garish red bedding salvia but it is actually a large and diverse group of useful plants. They are found worldwide but we shall mention here just a few that come from temperate areas and are tolerant of dry conditions.

Some of the most useful are the sages, all types of *S. officinalis*, (Z6) a small sub-shrub with aromatic foliage, and well known as a culinary herb. It has several cultivars such as 'Icterina' AGM with golden variegated foliage, 'Kew Gold' which has a lime green hue, 'Purpurascens' AGM with purple foliage and the lovely but slightly tender 'Tricolor'.

S. argentea (Z5) is herbaceous and makes a rosette of silver woolly foliage. It behaves as either a biennial or short-lived perennial and as soon as it flowers and seeds, has the disappointing habit of dying. Nevertheless it's a choice foliage plant. There are many other salvias, some of which may be worth trying but many of which are tender.

Santolina

Asteraceae/Compositae

These are familiar little cushion shaped shrubs from the Mediterranean, well know for their silver foliage and tolerance of hot dry conditions. Sometimes known as the cotton lavenders, they eventually have masses of small button-like flowers usually in yellow or white.

The most widely grown is *S. chamaecyparissus* AGM (Z7), which grows to about 45 cm (18 in) and has coarse yellow flower heads that add nothing to the value of the plant. By pruning hard each spring you can usually prevent the plant from flowering and keep it an tidy bun shape. 'Lemon Queen' has pale primrose flowers. A looser more upright form is often available, correctly called *S. pinnata* subsp *neapolitana*. Then there is *S. rosmarinifolia* syn *S. virens* with crisp green foliage and yellow flowers.

RIGHT Whilst playing the 'shrinking violet' for most of the year, *Stipa gigantea* suddenly becomes a total show-off with its exuberant display of golden seed heads.

GREEN ROOFS
In recent years, particularly in parts of Europe, it has become popular to surface roofs with a living carpet. These keep the building warm in winter and cool in summer as well as providing additional green living habitats in city areas. Sedums are often used to create these green roofscapes and not only grow in a very shallow layer of growing medium but require almost no maintenance.

Sedum

Crassulaceae

Next we have a genus of generally low growing succulent species, most of which are mat-forming perennials. They have very fleshy polished leaves and originate from mountainous and arid areas. Many are diminutive in stature and highly suitable for rock gardens.

One of the most recognisable is *S. acre*, (Z3) the common stonecrop. It is a very prostrate perennial with evergreen foliage growing to no more than 5 cm (2 in) in height but spreading up to 60 cm (2 ft) across and eventually more as it slowly creeps and roots. In mid summer it is covered with starry yellow flowers. *S. lydium* is a good companion for it, again mat-forming but with foliage that is tipped reddish bronze. My third selection in this group is *S. obtusatum* syn *rubroglaucum*, which has small rosettes of fleshy foliage, that turn a burnished red in cold weather. Finally *S. spathulifolium* 'Purpureum' AGM, (Z6) is worth growing with succulent silver foliage, suffused with rich purple.

Amongst the taller herbaceous perennials, we have S. spectabile AGM, (Z4) the ice plant, which grows to around 45 cm (18 in). The foliage is a bluish green and succulent.

Flowering takes place in late summer with brilliant pink flowers that attract bees and butterflies. The cultivar 'Iceberg' has white flowers, and 'Herbstfreude' syn 'Autumn Joy' AGM, has rich deep pink flowers. 'Ruby Glow' AGM, has not only rich ruby red flowers but also dark wine red foliage. All sedums are very tolerant of hot dry conditions.

Sempervivum

Crassulaceae

This is another group of related succulents that are easy to grow. They originate from mountainous parts of Europe. Traditionally they were often grown on the roofs of houses with the superstitious belief that they had the ability to protect a house from lightening. They all make tight rosettes of very fleshy, pointed leaves and some of them have a cobweb-like covering of fine white hairs, which adds to the beauty. After flowering, each rosette dies but they regularly produce new offsets which maintain the clump or can be used for propagation.

The common houseleek is called *S. tectorum* AGM, (Z3) and has rosettes around 10 cm (4 in) across of green leaves sometimes tinged with red. It produces spikes of pink flowers in summer. The cultivar 'Commander Hay' AGM has blood red tinged leaves and greenish red flowers. *S. arachnoideum* AGM, is the cobweb houseleek and has small rosettes thickly webbed with white hairs. There are many other named cultivars and species. All are good plants for a rock garden, the crevices in paving or for growing in shallow pans. They are extremely tolerant of dry conditions.

RIGHT The prostrate form of Rosemary will follow whatever surfaces it grows over, making delightful green 'steps' in even the driest of situations.

Senecio

Asteraceae/Compositae

This is a huge genus of plants found worldwide in a wide range of conditions. We will just describe a few sun lovers here.

S. cineraria (Z8) is the common silver leaved bedding plant, sometimes called dusty miller. It is available in a number of cultivars such as 'Silver Dust' AGM, with finely cut foliage and 'Cirrus', which has broader pure white leaves. Both grow to about 30 cm (1 ft) are amongst the most drought tolerant of bedding plants. The species *S. viraviva* syn *leucostachys* (Z9) makes a small open shrub around 60 cm (2 ft) tall with delicate filigree silver foliage.

Spartium

Leguminosae/Papilionaceae

Here we've got just one species that comes from dry scrubby roadsides and light woodland in parts of the Mediterranean. Commonly known as Spanish broom, *S. junceum* AGM, (Z8) is a useful shrub growing eventually to
3 m (10 ft) although it is more likely to sprawl and flop before it reaches this height. The stems are green and leaves are very sparse. In mid summer it rewards us with a spectacular display of rich yellow pea-like flowers. It can be pruned quite hard in the spring which will keep the plant compact but delay the flowering.

Stachys

Labiatae/Lamiaceae

Although a large group of plants, they come from varying habitats so only some are appropriate to include here. Most are herbaceous perennials.

PLANTING TIP

Use *Stachys* 'Primrose Heron' as a foil for a bright orange red hot poker such as 'Bees' Sunset' and compliment this with a background of purple foliage from *Cotinus coggygria* 'Atropurpurea'.

The most familiar is the cottage garden favourite, *S. byzantina* syn. *S. lanata* (Z5) more commonly known as lamb's ear. This forms a mat of soft velvety silver foliage that on close inspection can be seen to be covered with white hairs. It somewhat spoils its foil effect by sending up straggly flower spikes in mid summer with rather bland, pinkish purple flowers. It is prone to mildew but otherwise undemanding and tolerant of hot dry locations. There is a rather unusual form called 'Primrose Heron' with soft yellowish green leaves. If flower is more important to you, grow *S. macrantha*, (Z6) which has green leaves with bold chunky spikes of purplish-pink flowers produced in late spring.

Stipa

Poaceae

Another group of fabulous and fashionable grasses coming originally from rocky areas and prairies in various temperate regions. These are clump forming grasses so unlikely to become a nuisance in most gardens.
The most spectacular is *S. gigantea* AGM (Z6), golden oat grass. It makes large evergreen clumps of narrow grey-green leaves topped with huge heads of glittering bronze and gilt oat-like flowers. It grows to as much as 1.8 m (6 ft). Flowering commences in mid summer but the subsequent seedheads last well into

THYME LAWNS

We have already spoken about grass not always being successful or appropriate in a waterwise garden and it may be that thyme is more useful for a small green carpet. Thyme will make a low, fine-textured, green blanket that will visually look similar to a grass lawn but with the added bonus of flowers in early summer. A thyme lawn will take some foot traffic but not heavy wear. Suitable types would be cultivars of the very prostrate *T. serpyllum* such as:

'Annie Hall' – purple-pink
'Coccineus' AGM – crimson
'Pink Chintz' AGM, - flesh pink
'Snowdrift' – white

These will all produce a quite even low surface. There is no reason why some of the other slightly taller, bushier types cannot be used but the effect will be more undulating. The soils for thyme lawn should be as weed free as possible. The areas should be prepared well in advance and any weeds or grasses that appear hoed off or treated with glyphosate. The young thyme plants should be spaced about 15–20 cm apart (6–9 in). They will need watering in and some irrigation during establishment but once mature will remain green through most dry spells.

When in flower, bees will be attracted, necessitating caution when walking over the area. After flowering the lawn may need a very light trim to remove dead flower heads and tidy up. In a small area this can be by a pair of shears. On a larger area a hover mower, set very carefully, could be used.

the winter. It makes a good specimen amongst lower planting. Then we have *S. tenuissima*, (Z6) the pony tail grass, which is somewhat less spectacular, but still worth growing. It comes in much shorter at 75 cm (30 in) and has feathery flowers hanging like small waterfalls in mid summer that start green and fade to a pale straw colour. This one is best planted in drifts amongst other perennials such as the broad leaved Bergenia 'Abendglut'.

Tamarix

Tamaricaceae

The tamarisks are large shrubs or straggly trees that will put up with a wide range of conditions including drought and salt spray in windy seaside locations. The most familiar in temperate areas is *T. tetrandra* AGM (Z6). For most of the year it is an uninspiring plant with delicate feathery green foliage, a good background or screening plant. However in early

summer it bursts out in a froth of pale pink blossoms. I grew it once as a hedge behind black railings. Each year it grew out between the bars, softening them with a haze of green and pale pink. After flowering it was cut back to the railings.

Tanacetum

Asteraceae/Compositae

Another genus with some useful silver foliage plants. In most cases, the foliage has a pungent aroma. Despite its lengthy & cumbersome name, *T. densum* subsp *amani* (Z7) is a diminutive little plants with finely cut silver foliage. It makes a low carpet topped in summer with sparse yellow flowers that add little to the display. *T. ptarmiciflorum* is a sort of sub-shrub that can be propagated from cuttings. It grows to around 60 cm (2 ft) with feathery silver foliage. Both are drought tolerant.

Teucrium

Labiatae/Lamiaceae

Although a large genus, very few are regularly grown in gardens. They are mostly aromatic and come from scrubby, rocky areas, particularly in the Mediterranean. The most useful for us is the shrubby germander, *T. fruticans* (Z7). This is a rather lanky shrub with white furry square shoots and small grey-green leaves that are white underneath. Pinching when young and regular pruning will keep it compact, or it can be grown against a wall and the longer shoots tied in to a trellis or wires. In early summer, it produces pale blue flowers. There is an improved form , 'Azureum' AGM, with darker blue flowers.

LEFT Many people do not realise that *Trachycarpus fortunei* is a totally hardy palm and tolerant of many varying conditions including drought.

Thymus

Labiatae/Lamiaceae

Most of the thymes are natives of the Mediterranean, coming from dry grassy areas. They are nearly all low growing, and sometimes carpet forming shrubs and sub-shrubs. Most are aromatic and some have valuable culinary use as well as having attractive foliage and flower. There are many species and cultivars, which are often muddled in their naming.

The common culinary thyme is *T. vulgaris* (Z6), which makes a small spreading bush covered in tiny evergreen leaves. Bright purple flowers are produced in late spring. When growning for culinary use, trim regularly to encourage strong new shoots rather than flower.

T. citriodorus (Z6), the lemon thyme, is another good one. The cultivars *T. c.* 'Aureus' with gold foliage and *T.c.* 'Silver Queen' AGM are the most commonly grown of the species. 'Aureus' has particularly rich gold foliage and makes a good reliable splash of bright winter colour.

Then we have *T. serpyllum* (Z5), which is a very low mat forming species that hugs the ground. There are many cultivars such as 'Pink Chintz' AGM and 'Snowdrift'. The range of colours within the thymes includes most shades from white, through pale and dark pink to almost rose red.

Trachycarpus

Arecaceae/Palmae

This genus includes one of the few palms that are truly frost hardy. *T. fortunei* (Z7), AGM, the Chusan palm comes from subtropical Asia and is tough and trouble free. It produces the typical fan of dark green leaves from a single stem. Old specimens can eventually get to

20 m (70 ft) but growth is very slow, so they are unlikely to be a problem. Mature specimens may produce yellow flowers followed by attractive, blue-black fruit. They also grow well in a large pot or tub as patio specimens. This palm is a real 'hardy exotic' giving a touch of the tropics to any garden.

Tulip

Liliaceae

A group of well known bulbs that originate from hot dry areas in Europe, Asia and the middle east. Like many bulbs, they survive the heat of the summer by becoming dormant and only the underground bulb survives, protected from the extremes of heat by the covering soil. Re-growth and flowering occurs in the cooler and moister months of the year. Over the centuries tulips have been highly hybridised and rare ones greatly valued. The result is that there are now many hundreds of different cultivars. These are classified into different groups to make naming easier.

The so-called botanical tulips include a number of early flowering type such as *T. kaufmanniana*, the water lily tulip, which opens to a bowl-shaped flower. Later tulips include the lily-flowered types with pointed petals, the parrot groups with striped petals and the hybrid groups such as Darwin and Triumph tulips, which are widely used for bedding. Although all tulips will grow in hot dry conditions, probably some of the best will be the actual species such as *T. greigii*, *T. acuminata*, *T. sprengeri*, *T. tarda* and *T. turkestanica*. These are worth searching out from a specialist bulb merchant for specific spring colours. While tulips can vary a little most are zone 4.

Ulex

Leguminosae/Papilionaceae

This genus includes the common gorse, native to the UK and many parts of Europe as well as N. Africa. These come from heaths, rocky hillsides and woodland margins and are all very drought tolerant. The common gorse is *U. europaeus* (Z7) but the form 'Flore Pleno' is a better garden plant with double yellow flowers that do not set seed. The main flush of flower is in late spring and early summer but there is spasmodic flowering throughout the year. Hence the phrase 'when the gorse is out of bloom, kissing is out of season!' Dense bushes have spiny green shoots and tiny leaves that are also modified into spines. Although it tolerates extreme drought very well, it also burns well so can be a fire hazard when very dry.

Verbascum

Scrophulariaceae

The mulleins are a group of plants that produce brightly coloured spires of flower. Wild species come from poor stony ground in parts of Europe and Turkey. Many are biennials and those that are perennial are often short-lived. These really do thrive in hot dry situations. Wet soils tend to rot the roots so always ensure that drainage is good with some additional grit in the soil, particularly in areas such as the UK where winter rainfall is high.

V. olympicum (Z6) is a short-lived perennial with 1.5 m (5 ft) spikes of yellow flowers over a rosette of greyish leaves. The other common species is *V. phoeniceum* (Z6) with somewhat shorter spikes of purplish flowers. Recent interest has resulted in a flurry of new cultivars both from the UK and overseas. 'Helen Johnson' is a wonderful soft caramel in colour but sadly short-lived. The Cotswold hybrids are generally all worth growing, including the cultivar 'Gainsborough' AGM which has sulphur yellow flowers.

There are many good ones but also some inferior seed raised strains so choose with care. One reliable seed-raised hybrid is called 'Arctic Summer' and makes lovely chunky rosettes of pure silver foliage in its first season. If kept until the second year it will produce spires of yellow flowers but these are of poor quality, so it is best regarded as a good silver-leaved bedding plant and thrown at the end of the summer.

BELOW Amongst the many verbenas, one of the most floriferous is the old cultivar 'Sissinghurst' which thrives on drought and neglect, producing masses of brilliant cerise flowers whatever the weather.

Verbena
Verbenaceae

Most people would recognise verbenas as familiar bedding plants but there are a number that are perennial and very tolerant of hot dry conditions. They are mainly natives of dry areas of tropical and subtropical America but many have proved amazingly tough and hardy. There are both some tall slender types and also low growing ground hugging sorts.

V. bonariense AGM (Z8) is one of the taller types reaching to 90 cm (3 ft) with willowy stems carrying small heads of purplish pink flowers. It is sometimes grown as a constituent if prairie plantings, where it will self-seed and appear all over the place. Its one of those useful filigree plants which provide

height in a planting but are thin enough that they do not block a view – you can see through them! The late Christopher Lloyd loved it within his jungle garden, where it mixed with cannas, dahlias and all manner of exotics.

Amongst the lower growing types we have *V. peruviana* (Z7) which is really a quite diminutive plant suitable for a rock garden, making a small mat with bright red flowers. There is also a good, free-flowering white form. Some of the bedding types will last from year to year if given a warm spot and good drainage and will make sizeable clumps covered in summer flower. The rich cerise 'Sissinghurst', the paler pink 'Silver Anne', which is also deliciously scented and *V. tennusisecta*, a good blue, are all worth trying.

Yucca
Agavaceae

Yet another spiky and a very useful one, as many species are totally hardy and yet they seem to really typify desert planting. Most come from hot dry areas of central and north America. All have wonderful architectural outlines of lance-shaped leaves from a central rosette and a bonus of spectacular spikes of usually white bell-shaped flowers. Most are monocarpic, which means that when they flower, the main shoot will die, although this is usually replaced by offsets produced around the mother plant.

Y. filamentosa AGM (Z5) is clump-forming with dark green leaves adorned with curly white threads and grows to about 75cm (30in). The flowering stem, which appears in late summer will shoot up to around 1.8 m (6 ft). 'Variegata' AGM has white margins and 'Bright Edge' AGM has very rich golden edges to the leaves but is less vigorous.

Another good species is *Y. flaccida* (Z5), also with clumps of green leaves. As the name would suggest, the leaves are not so rigid. The cultivar 'Ivory' AGM is probably the best one to grow for its creamy flowers, which are produced in great profusion on a huge spike in late summer, often lasting well into the autumn. 'Golden Sword' AGM is another good yellow variegated type but once again less vigorous than the species.

Y. gloriosa AGM (Z7) makes short branched stems, which with time give the plant a short, stocky tree-like appearance. The rosettes of leaves are attached to the top of each stem. Flowering is again in late summer and there is also a good form called 'Variegata' AGM with yellow margins.

Zauschneria
Onagraceae

Its always comforting in an A-Z book to have a genuine Z plant to finish the sequence with! In this case *Zauschneria* is a valid inclusion. Known as the Californian fuchsia, this comes from hot dry slopes in western north America. These are sub-shrubs with brittle stems and delicate green leaves that light up with brightly coloured flowers.

Z. californica AGM is the common species flowering in late summer with tubular orange red flowers. The cultivars 'Dublin' AGM and 'Western Hills' both have deep red flowers. There is also a white form 'Albiflora' and a pink form ' Solidarity Pink'. All are on the borderline of hardiness so plant in a well drained warm, sheltered spot where they will tolerate reasonably dry conditions.

RIGHT Growing amongst a groundcover ivy, *Yucca* 'Golden Sword' provides the perfect spiky contrast with both plants being very tolerant of low water.

What not to grow

The following list includes a number of garden favourites which need to be irrigated in dry seasons and require a moist soil to grow and thrive. For this reason they are best avoided in the waterwise garden.

Acer species – maples
Acorus – rushes
Adiantum – maidenhair fern
Aquilegia – columbine
Arundo – giant reed
Asplenium – ferns
Aster – Michaelmas daisy
Astilbe
Begonia
Betula – birches
Buxus – box
Calluna – Scot's heather
Caltha – marsh marigold
Camellia
Campanulas – bellflowers
Cannas – Indian shot plants
Carex – sedges
Chamaecyparis – cypress
Chrysanthemum
Clematis
Dahlia
Daphne
Davidia – handkerchief tree
Delphineum
Dicentra – bleeding heart
Digitalis – foxglove
Ensete – false banana
Epimedium

Eremurus – foxtail lily
Erica – heathers
Forsythia
Fritillaria – crown imperials
Fuchsia
Galanthus – snowdrops
Gentiana – gentian
Geranium – cranesbills
Gunnera – aquatic plant
Hamamelis – witchhazel
Helleborus – hellebores, including
   Christmas roses
Hemerocallis – day lilies
Hosta – plantain lilies
Hydrangea
Ilex – holly
Impatiens – busy Lizzie
Jasminum – jasmine
Lilium – lilies
Liquidambar
Liriodendron – tulip tree
Lobelia
Lonicera – honeysuckle
Magnolia
Malus – ornamental crabs and apples
Meconopsis
Mimulus – musk
Muscari – grape hyacinth
Narcissus – daffodils
Osmanthus
Paeonia – peony
Phlox – herbaceous types
Pieris
Pleione – hardy orchid
Primula – including primrose and polyanthus

Prunus – cherries, ornamental and fruiting
Pulmonaris – lungwort
Rheum – ornamental rhubarbs
Rhododendron – including azaleas
Ribes – flowering currant
Rosa – roses
Salix – willows
Saxifraga – saxifrage
Skimmia
Sorbus – rowans and whitebeams
Spiraea
Syringa – lilac
Tilia – limes
Typha – bulrush
Viburnums
Vinca – periwinkle
Viola – pansies and violas
Vitis – grape and ornamental vines
Wisteria

A list such as this can never be totally definitive and your experiences of plants that will and won't tolerate drought conditions may vary from mine. Experimenting with plants in your garden's own unique conditions is the only way to truly establish if a plant will thrive. However, it may be useful to use this list as a guide to which plants are unlikely to survive in a waterwise garden.

List of terms

Arid – climates that are extremely dry and lacking in moisture.

Drainage – the movement of excess water down through the soil.

Drought – defined as a period of time when there is not enough water to support farming, urban, human, and environmental water needs.

Exotic – strictly speaking this refers to any plant which is not native to the area, but popularly it is used to describe unusual or striking plants.

Glaucous – a plant's surfaces, often leaves, covered with a silvery bluish-grey bloom that helps retain moisture.

Grey water – non-industrial wastewater produced by domestic processes such as washing dishes, laundry and bathing. Greywater comprises 50-80 per cent of residential wastewater. Greywater gets its name from its cloudy appearance and from its status as being neither fresh nor heavily polluted. Greywater is distinct from blackwater, which is basically sewage.

Irrigation – the artificial application of water to the soil, mainly used to replace missing rainfall in periods of drought.

Microclimate – small areas where the climate is slightly different from the overall surroundings. Often used to refer to particular parts of a garden.

Mulch – any loose material placed over the soil to act as a protective covering, reducing water loss and discouraging weeds.

Pan – a hard layer within the soil that impedes drainage and interrupts root growth.

Precipitation – any form of water, rain, snow, sleet or hail that is deposited on the earth's surface.

Succulent – a type of plants that has fleshy leaves, stems or roots and is able to store water.

Temperate – in geographical terms, temperate areas of the world lie between the tropics and the polar circles. The changes in these regions between summer and winter are generally subtle (warm or cool), rather than extreme (burning hot or freezing cold). However, a temperate climate can have very unpredictable weather.

Transpiration – the loss of water through the pores of the leaf.

Xeriscape – landscaping in ways that do not require supplemental irrigation. The term Xeriscaping was coined by combining the words *xeros* (Greek for 'dry') and landscape.

APPENDIX

Useful contacts

The following websites contain useful advice and equipment suggestions for the waterwise gardener.

Access Irrigation Ltd
www.access-irrigation.net
Supplier of Irrigation equipment.

Aquastore
www.water-recycling-filter.com
Grey water filtration systems.

Clearwell Rainpiper
www.clearwell-rainpiper.co.uk
Vertical rainwater storage systems.

Hozelock Limited
www.hozelock.com
Supplier of irrigation equipment.

Klargester
www.klargester.com/products/raintrap/index.htm
Internatiional suppliers of underwater household storage tanks.

Raincatch
www.raincatch.com
Rainwater harvesting systems.

Rainharvesting Systems
www.rainharvesting.co.uk
Commercial organization offering rainwater storage systems. Systems suitable for household as well as garden use.

Rainwater Harvesting Association
http://www.ukrha.org
Advice on harvesting and re-using rainwater.

Royal Horticultural Society
www.rhs.org.uk/learning/research/
conservation_and_environment_water.asp
Advice on waterwise gardening.

Water Guide Organisation
www.water-guide.org.uk
General guidance on water usage.

Waterwise Organisation
www.waterwise.org.uk
Water saving advice including waterwise gardening.

Index

INDEX

INDEX

Picture credits

Ian Cooke

pages 11, 26, 33, 36, 40, 47, 56, 57, 59, 60, 61, 63, 70, 76, 77, 78, 82, 83, 85, 92, 94, 99, 101, 102, 107, 109, 111, 113, 115, 117, 118, 121, 123, 125, 127, 129, 131, 133, 135, 137, 143, 147, 149, 151, 153, 155, 157, 159, 160, 163, 164, 167, 169, 171, 172, 175, 177, jacket back cover.

Photos Horticultural

7, 23, 29, 49, 51, 54, 65, 68, 90, 185, 192.

Garden Picture Library

2, 8, 13, 15, 17, 31, 38, 42, 45, 50, 53, 67, 73, 80, 88, 89, 93, 96, 105, 139, 141, 145, 181, 183, jacket front cover.